"The plight of Western Ukrainians who were forcibly de[...] to distant regions of the Soviet Union is one of the lesser [...] in the tragic tapestry of World War II. *In Woman* [...] in a fine English translation by Marie Chm[...] Starosolska affords the reader a windo[...] whose life was buffeted by the world-hi[...] ntieth century. Starosolska's vignettes of her orde[...] a mosaic of loss, love, and laughter, and her memoir is a [...]y to the resilience of the human spirit."

Peter L. Rudnytsky,
University of Florida

"In this beautifully written and sensitively translated memoir, Juliana Starosolska takes the reader on a fascinating journey through her oftentimes harrowing experiences as a political deportee in war-time Soviet Kazakhstan. Although the violence and brutality of the Communist regime are always in the background, Starosolska manages to find humanity in her many encounters with fellow exiles and local Kazakhs—proving in the final analysis that inhuman regimes can never extinguish the human spirit."

Alexander J. Motyl,
Rutgers University

"This book will take you on the journey of an extraordinary woman, Juliana Starosolska. Raised in the midst of key events and intellectual trends in the twentieth century Western Ukraine, her family like so many other nationally conscious Ukrainian families during the Stalinist years was arrested, separated, deported, subjected to deprivation and abuses, the father disappearing without a trace in a prison camp. Yet Juliana evokes optimism. Forced to endure unimaginable horrors, she retains a strong feeling of humanity, dignity, respect for others, and a sense of humour."

Marta Dyczok,
University of Western Ontario

WOMAN IN EXILE

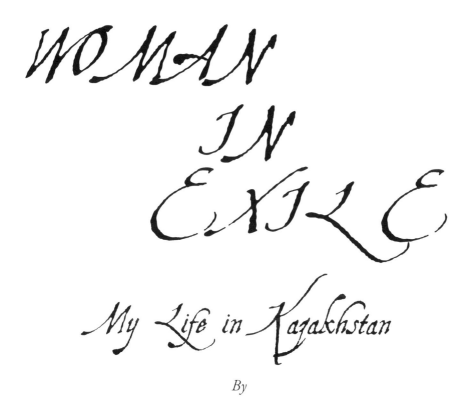

WOMAN IN EXILE

My Life in Kazakhstan

By

Juliana Starosolska

Translated by

Marie Chmilewsky Ulanowicz

iUniverse, Inc.
Bloomington

Woman in Exile
My Life in Kazakhstan

iUniverse books may be ordered through booksellers or by contacting:

iUniverse
1663 Liberty Drive
Bloomington, IN 47403
www.iuniverse.com
1-800-Authors (1-800-288-4677)

ISBN: 978-1-4620-0371-6 (sc)
ISBN: 978-1-4620-0373-0 (dj)
ISBN: 978-1-4620-0372-3 (ebk)

Library of Congress Control Number: 2011906654

Printed in the United States of America

iUniverse rev. date: 4/28/2011

Contents

Foreword

With the signing of the Molotov-Ribbentrop Pact on August 24, 1939 by the USSR and Nazi Germany, the way was paved for the Soviet invasion of Western Ukraine of September 17, 1939. After the end of World War I, Ukraine had been partitioned by the Treaty of Versailles, with the east being absorbed by the Soviet Union and the west annexed to Poland. Now the invasion reunited, but also redefined, the country as the Ukrainian Soviet Socialist Republic.

Within six months of the invasion, the Soviets were arresting, executing, imprisoning and deporting leading Ukrainian, Polish and Jewish citizens on a massive scale. The author of these memoirs, Juliana Starosolska, is the daughter of a prominent Ukrainian lawyer and scholar who was taken with the very first wave of these arrests. He was sentenced, as an "enemy of the people" to a GULAG deep in the heart of Siberia, where he eventually perished. On April 13th 1940, the rest of his family still living in Ukraine—the author, her mother and one of her brothers—were forcibly deported from Ukraine. They were given less than an hour to pack their belongings, then locked in a box car with similar misfortunates and transported thousands of miles to the extreme eastern corner of Kazakhstan.

Kazakhstan is the ninth largest country in the world, about four times the size of Texas. Historically the native population had been overwhelmingly nomadic, although from the 19th century until the disintegration of the Soviet Union it was governed by a colonialist Russian minority—first as part of the tsarist Russian empire and then as one of the republics of the Soviet Union. In 1991, Kazakhstan declared independence; it was the last of the Soviet republics to do so.

Kazakhstan is the largest landlocked country in the world. Far from the moderating influence of any sea, its climate is continental and arid, with extremely hot, but short, summers and brutally cold, long winters. The Soviet government, determined to develop the country's vast agricultural and mineral potential, sought to accomplish that transformation by harnessing the Soviet Union's enormous mass of political prisoners into an expendable labor force.

These are the circumstances into which Juliana Starosolska and her family were thrust, and this is her story.

Marie Chmilewsky Ulanowicz
September 29, 2009
Gainesville, Florida

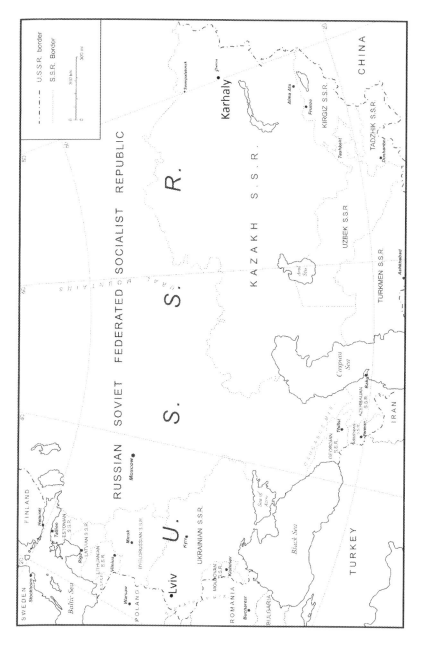

USSR ca.1940. Lviv, Ukraine (near extreme left); Karhaly, Kazakhstan (far right).

Introduction

Like a Rip Van Winkle who found himself in his home village after decades of sleep, so I too find myself, after 27 years, among my family, my dear friends and my acquaintances. Here they stand before me with their children, some even with grandchildren. Some, perhaps, had already crossed me off from their list of memories, perhaps not even counting me among the living. They all greet me as someone who has come to them from a distant planet. That which binds us is a shared youth. That which divides us is not only elapsed time, but also wholly different events, layer upon layer of experiences, pain, and emotions blanketing the mind and soul.

Just imagine! Here is my brother. I remember him last, when 27 years ago, in the dark of night I walked him out to the street corner by the Lviv Polytechnic Institute. The rain poured and tears ran down my young face– it was a premonition of our long separation. My brother was being forced to leave Lviv.

Now he meets me at the airport. I recognize him from afar. He doesn't seem that much older, only different. And I notice that he is gazing at me intently, as if I were someone he must come to know anew.

And this woman--- she's my friend from our scouting days. I last saw her wearing heavy hiking boots, carrying a backpack up Mt. Syvulia. Now, she is still slim, only her hair color has changed somewhat and she's wearing high heels as she runs up to me, smiling through her tears.

And this fair-haired young lady next to her is smiling as well (of course she's smiling, she's had a proper upbringing!) and yet, somehow, she seems indifferent—that's her daughter. She is now her mother's age when together we climbed Mt. Syvulia.

And this man with his thick grey thatch of hair, who wonders how it is that I haven't grayed in spite of "having lived through so much." (How dare my hair not turn grey when his did!) He was once a youth. He once strolled with me down the streets of Lviv, or through Striyskiy Park, spouting extravagantly impassioned ideas, which in his opinion could lead the world onto new paths. Now he worries about his son, who has grown a beard and walks the streets of New York, barefoot.

And this young man? Can this be Vlodko, whose pram I pushed through Yezuyitsky Park? Now he has come out from California to meet me, and I struggle to recognize him from his pictures. He is a head taller than me and as I walk with him, I notice that girls are ogling him. (It's true, back in "our" days girls did it more discreetly!) He hugs me, his "new" aunt, gently patting my back.

"One more aunt! Good God, how many there are!"

I might go on listing the entire group of people who have come out to meet me as if I were some extraterrestrial. Together with me, they once trembled at the sound of the doorbell or a nighttime knock, lest it be the Polish security police. Together with me, they wandered down country roads that wound their way about my heart like a golden serpent. Perhaps, some had been in love with me, writing poetic love letters. After all, it is said that it's the unfulfilled kind of love that is ideal.

Perhaps they were my "until-death-do-us-part" friends. Our friendships, interrupted by fate, were in full bloom then, undulled by everyday cares, unexposed to the tests of adversity and the violence of war, but, at the same time, untouched by the good fortune and the prosperity that destroy just as readily.

They greet me. But it's not me at whom they smile, not the "now" me, not that me which life molded, ground down, and then remolded. They smile at our shared youth. In their minds I am as I used to be, because I did not experience the German occupation with them, nor the evacuations, nor the Displaced Persons camps, nor the hardships of emigration. I couldn't—I wasn't there with them. Between the time that I last saw them and now, there is an enormous void. For them I am a continuation of their youth. Their conversations with me begin most often with "Do you remember...?"

Of course, I remember. It's this memory of mine that has allowed me to survive so much. Maybe that's why my hair has not turned grey yet; my memory and I are bound so tightly to our youth. Yet time not only passed, time bore its own events. I did not sleep like Rip Van Winkle.

Actually, the issue is not simply the experienced past. All these dear people whom I now meet lived through their own uncertain, hard years together. They were bound together by the same customs, the same laws of communal life. If their way of thinking changed, it changed under the same circumstances. There, where I had been, not only the landscape, the climate and the people, but even the rules governing human behavior were different. What sets us apart most is that ongoing struggle for life without a concurrent loss of one's humanity. What a tremendous "re-evaluation of priorities" had to take place in an environment where such an alien value—indeed, no value at all—is placed on human life. What meaning could religion have for people who long ago forgot or never even learned how to bless themselves? Who had only vaguely heard of Christ? Where any sense of ethnic or national consciousness was, in itself, proof of a dangerously independent, willful, free thinking?

You probably think too that somehow I'm a little strange, that I've changed. Not just externally—obviously—but you must be amazed that I am unable to understand or take part in some of your discussions, arguments and misunderstandings, which I simply cannot and do not wish to comprehend.

I think, perhaps, that if I could tell you something about myself—no, not only about myself—if I could tell you something about us, those who were deported far to the east, to the distant corners of Kazakhstan and Siberia in April of 1940, if I could only show you a tiny bit, bring you a little closer to that land of bleak wintriness, then perhaps we might understand each other better.

Returning in my mind to those times, people and events appear in a vision before me, coming together like frames in a film. So come, take a look at these images of life "over there." Perhaps then, that time-void which stands between us will be filled, so I can become something more than a mere shadow or a reflection of your youth, more than a brief and pleasant interlude before you continue on your way.

Perhaps then, in that thin wall which I sense hanging between us, that partition erected by others, made up of differing life experiences, there can spring forth new golden threads that can bind us into a mutual acceptance, understanding and closeness. I do not want to remain among you merely as a woman of "those" times, a distant figure in your memory, an insignificant trace of years past.

Chapter 1:

In the Boxcar

I have a recurring nightmare. Each time there's a slight variation in the detail, but the circumstances are always the same and I wake up, paralyzed in fear, sometimes drenched in a cold sweat, and for a long time I lie motionless. I'm too terrified to open my eyes; I'm afraid that instead of the familiar surroundings, the outline of the window, the book shelves, the glint of the mirror, I will see the bowels of a railroad boxcar filled with dozing figures, huddled everywhere. Lying there in a panic, before I dare open my eyes, I first make certain that the sound, which in my dream was the monotonous clacking of train wheels, is really the sound of some appliance in the apartment overhead or perhaps the rumble of trucks in the street. The sharp, piercing whistle of a Soviet locomotive, a sound unlike any that I have ever heard, echoing always like a curse or a cry of despair, fades with the dream. I listen to the familiar sounds of a big city and slowly force my heart to relax. My thoughts, nonetheless, keep returning to that boxcar, to which we—my mother, my brother and I—were taken on that ill-fated morning of Friday the thirteenth, April 1940.

At first it seemed that the boxcar could not possibly fit any more people, crammed as it already was with people and packages. Nevertheless we boarded and squeezed our way in with our wicker trunk that had so often accompanied us on our happy holidays to Pidliute. Then, it held linens, dishes and books. Now, we weren't exactly sure what it contained because we were given less than twenty minutes to pack. We filled the trunk with whatever was at hand, whatever caught our eye; there was no time to choose between things that might be useful. We shoved the trunk into the boxcar, thinking that it might possibly serve as a cot for our mother, since all the berths had already been taken. We managed to secure a spot for her next to the trunk, where she could sit on the smaller bundles.

In my dream the boxcar always appears to me as it was at night. Maybe that's because at night each of us sank deep into ourselves, into our own thoughts. At night the car was loaded with fifty human tragedies. During the day people reclaimed their voices, reclaimed their identities as physical beings, with physical needs to eat, drink, and to breathe, (yes, because even the air seemed rationed). But at night all the bodies seemed to melt into the darkness of the boxcar. Each one of us would arrange ourselves as comfortably as we could for the night but it was probably only the children who slept deeply, secure in their slumber. The rest were rarely blessed with such sweet oblivion. Despair, worry and sorrow took over. They filled the car with a nearly palpable mist, a dark veil, like threads of a cobweb creeping from one huddled figure to the next. Even as I slept I could sense this plasma of fear, this tacky fog that emerged at night from the depths of human souls.

Sometimes, the soft whispers of two figures might be heard as they leaned into one another. Somewhere someone sobbed. Someone else murmured prayers, or maybe, while in half-sleep, conversed with a phantom being.

Because—suddenly—Fate had split in two the lives of all who were in that boxcar. All matters, important and unimportant, all carefully constructed plans were slashed when a pitiless force seized them all at night and hurled them into this boxcar. Until that moment, everyone had gone to sleep with some assurance of a tomorrow and now that tomorrow was gone. Matters of love, hate, anger, hurt, ordinary troubles and joys—all these were left behind, outside the sealed boxcar. Now it was too late to repair or alter those final words spoken in anger. Apprehension about the future mingled with a regret for the past and an anxiety about those left behind—with a longing to see them just one more time, to speak just one more word, to do just one more thing.

During those initial moments in the boxcar, people acted as if in a hypnotic trance. Everyone seemed oblivious of everyone else, thinking only to claim a space for themselves and for their loved ones. Amid the general desperate bustle, everything revolved around the self. The thoughts and emotions of those who were being locked in were not focused on the underlying reality of the boxcar doors slamming shut. Instead they thought about petty matters: their little bundles, a place to sit. Some subconscious instinct seemed to make people turn to the minutiae of physical existence so as to drown out an essential and oppressive reality. This bustling, nervous activity seemed to come from an inner need to prove to ourselves that although we were being deported as prisoners, we were, in some way, still capable of acting as free individuals.

But possibilities for action in a packed boxcar are limited. Everything seemed, somehow, set. Still, it seemed terribly important to inspect the contents of our bundles. And so, again and again, almost everyone re-checked what they brought. And then, when even this task was completed and there was nothing else left to do, all defenses against the grim reality of the situation were lost.

Slowly, all of us, uprooted from our normal environment, began to create a new community—of people locked in a boxcar. Before, many things had both united and divided us. In our previous lives we were people of diverse nationalities, ages, faiths and occupations. Here, in the boxcar, our shared desire to arrange our common quarters as best we could also caused friction, because in this cramped space, we inevitably got in each other's way.

After the initial bustle, everyone tried to press through to the one tiny window to glimpse, at least, the outer world—to look at Lviv. There were many trains like ours standing at the freight station. They were visible to one side of us and we could see others, like us, peering through tiny windows of their own. To the other side we could make out the roofs of the townhouses of upper Horodetska Street.

So we sat there at the Lviv station, for maybe a day, maybe more. Time under such circumstances seems to acquire a different dimension. It seemed to us that as long as we could see a patch of sky over Lviv, there was still some hope. Something could happen, someone might intervene on our behalf, maybe they would let us go, maybe one of us might succeed in escaping. But we were guarded by armed soldiers. At night the cars were lit up with bright spotlights that lent a surreal quality to the entire area. Occasionally a shot was heard—maybe someone had tried to escape. Sometimes someone could be heard crawling beneath the railroad cars searching for family members. A name or surname was called and then repeated, from car to car, from train to train. The guards, however, quickly chased away such "visitors."

Suddenly, sounds of wailing and lamentation could be heard. One train after another began to move. The cries in the boxcars were echoed by the cries of people standing along the tracks, in the streets and on the embankments. This mournful wail that escorted the transports, now often comes to me in my dreams as the musical accompaniment to the nightmarish vision of the night in the boxcar.

I always see the boxcar at night. It may be that those physical depredations of hunger, lack of air, confinement, filth, and cold, although more difficult to bear at the time, left shallower scars than the horror of separation, the fear, and the despair that emerged when the black wings of night enveloped the people in the boxcar.

Chapter 2:
Hail, Kyiv! Farewell, Kyiv!

Our train, only one of many, circled Lviv and then swiftly headed east. It first passed through villages and towns whose names were familiar to us either because we personally had visited them or from stories of others who lived or visited there. We were always trying to find some way of getting word back to our relatives and friends. It seemed to be a matter of great importance for us. We dropped notes through the window to passers-by, even when the train was in motion. Occasionally we'd see someone pick up a note and then wave to us. Maybe, we thought, they would mail it home. But what home? We no longer had a home. Well then, if not to our home, then at least to our hometown—to our people.

When we reached Ternopil two people from each boxcar were allowed out to fetch water—under guard, of course. There was a huge crowd near the station's pump where we were allowed to draw water. We noticed looks of compassion, and we were peppered with questions, but no one was allowed to come near us. A railroad worker, taking advantage of a guard's momentary inattention, ran up to me and handed me a small package. Back in the car I saw that he had given me a lunch that his wife, no doubt, prepared for him to take to work. Two slices of bread with a sausage—what a touching gesture!

And then we traveled on. We came to the border—the former frontier. We entered the territory of Greater Ukraine[1], known to us only from legend and history; it was the home of our dreams. Only Mother had actually ever been here. Long ago she traveled here from Halychyna, smuggling contraband literature, when, as members of liberation organizations, our parents struggled against the tsarist regime. How different was her mode of travel now! She sat there in her little corner, resting her head, characteristically inclined on her hand. Her shining dark eyes, filled with quiet resignation, took on a look of despair only when she gazed at us. Her concern was only for us, never for herself.

The crossing of the border became apparent not only because the place names were now unfamiliar to us, the landscape changed as well. Poorly cultivated fields, grey, neglected buildings and shabbily dressed people who stared at us (and we them) were everywhere. Everything— people and structures—took on a characteristically gray complexion.

In Zhmerynka we took on water again. And here again, there was a crowd that stared at us. But these looks were marked more with curiosity than compassion. Once more I tried to pass along a postcard. Although we were well guarded, I walked past a young girl, close to my own age. She stood there eyeing us carefully. Taking advantage of the guard's momentary distraction I handed her my letter and asked, "Please buy some stamps and mail this letter."

The girl, noticing that I had given her some coins along with the letter, returned them to me and said, "Don't worry, I'll mail it!" Then she added, "And all of you stare at us as if we were some kind of wild beasts!" Surprised, I wanted to ask what she meant by that, but we were being herded on. For a long time I thought about her words. What was she thinking? Why would we possibly consider these people to be "wild beasts"? Was it because of their pathetically poor clothing, in contrast to ours? Or was it because, without a shot being fired, they invaded our homeland and were now behaving like "wild beasts" there? As I sat there locked in the freight boxcar, the words of this "free" girl continued to ring in my ears.

---

1   After the signing of the treaty of Versailles in 1919 Ukraine was divided territorially: Greater Ukraine became part of the Soviet Union; Western Ukraine, known by the regional name of Halychyna came under administrative control of Poland.

But here was Golden-domed Kyiv! My brother and I were finally lucky enough to make our way to the little window—usually so crowded by our fellow travelers. At last, it seemed, they recognized that we too had a right to look out the window.

I stood with my brother by the window, gazing. We were atop a bridge over a wide river. The sun was setting and in its golden light we saw the steep banks of the Dniepr River. The train crossed the bridge very slowly, barely moving. We caught sight of Volodymyr's Hill; we thought that maybe we could even make out the statue of St. Volodymyr. The sun gilded the church domes. We looked out at the capital of Ukraine, the city of our dreams, the city we so longed to see. The train paused momentarily in the middle of the bridge. A hush came over the boxcar. Wordlessly, silently, attentively we gazed, gorging ourselves on this magnificent, sun-gilded landscape. Hail Kyiv! Farewell Kyiv!

And then, ever onward, ever eastward! Where to? No one ever responded to our questions, not the guards who sometimes brought bread or let us out to fetch water, nor the people who walked past the train, nor the inhabitants of the towns and villages, whom we passed on our way to the water stations. There were so many people here, young and old, people with children, people with bundles. They stared at us, and we at them. Where were all these people going? Why were they on the move? Only later did we learn the reason behind this mass migration of peoples. In the Soviet Union life was hard everywhere and everyone was searching for a better place to live.

At a more extended stop, we saw another train with its locomotive stationed near our car. We called out to the train engineer, "Do you know where they're taking us? What will become of us?"

He pretended not to hear, but as soon as it was dark, he approached our window and asked who we were and where we had come from. When we explained that we were Ukrainians from Lviv, and that we are being deported to some unknown destination, he looked around to make sure there was no one nearby and said, "I don't know exactly where it is that they are taking you, but my own family, all of them, is somewhere out there. Don't despair, this can't last forever. There has to be an end to this misery."

He promised to find out about the destination of our train, but before he could return, our train moved on and we never saw him again.

The names of the small stations became meaningless to us now; we had never heard of any of them. And now, here were the Ural Mountains, somehow smaller than we had imagined. We all had known them only as a brown-colored chain of mountains on a map, beyond which Asia lay. Now Asia greeted us with a sandstorm. Long after the storm was over, even though we had tightly secured the tiny window, we continued to find sand in every nook of our boxcar, in our clothing and among our belongings.

Each day, breathing the air in the boxcar became more difficult. The small hole which was meant to serve as a toilet was simply a travesty. We had curtained it off with blankets and sheets, each one of us contributing as best we could, but it became impossible to keep clean and the increasingly noxious odors spread throughout the car because there was no water to wash off the boards around the hole.

Every morning began with the same girl's full-throttled voice, bellowing from the window of our neighboring car, "Water, water!" Sooner or later, the guards, having grown tired of listening to this persistent yelling, would then unlock the boxcars, one at a time, and let out two people from each car to fetch the water. The problem was, however, that there were no really suitable water containers. Sometimes the guards brought us bread. But not everyone respected it properly. Some still had food supplies from home and this heavy dark bread did not suit their tastes. Others had absolutely no food at all so we shared what we had with them. Somewhere beyond the Urals, children ran up to our tiny window and begged for... bread. This was a clear message for us all to appreciate the bread we had. What kind of future lay in store for us if these "free" people came to us to beg for bread?

Gradually we began to lose a sense of time; as we moved farther east, the time of sunrise and sunset changed; it became for us the measure of our eastward journey. Judging by the sun's position we reckoned that the train had changed direction: we were now heading south. We saw more mountains outside our little window, but what these were, we did not know.

We had been traveling for nearly three weeks when the train made a night stop and remained there longer than ever before. In the morning, as we rose from our sleep on the floorboards, we looked through our window to see the steppe, still covered with snow and depressing in its monotony. Only by peering very carefully were we able to make out houses. A wind blew carrying sand and pebbles played a tune on the telephone poles. From other boxcars we heard the clanging of doors opening; at first the sound came from far away, then closer and closer, finally reaching our neighboring car. At last our own door opened. We had arrived at our destination.

Chapter 3:

A Human Being, Writ Large

The long lines of freight trains continued to stand parallel to Horodetska Street at the Lviv Railroad depot all night as trucks kept pulling up to the trains, hauling in people to be deported. An elderly lady, brought into the boxcar almost simultaneously with us, was carried in on an armchair. Another woman followed her, weeping and carrying old-fashioned bags and suitcases. These two became our neighbors on this road to hell.

How this semi-paralyzed little old lady could possibly have posed any threat to the Soviet Union was surely beyond anyone's comprehension. Maybe someone wanted her living quarters or perhaps she was related to someone who had been arrested. No one cared whether she was young or old, frail or healthy. She was simply something on some list that had to be attended to—and checked off. But the woman who was brought in together with the elderly lady was another matter altogether.

She was a nurse. It was her job to care for the old lady. When the Red Army soldiers, armed with clubs and guns, entered the apartment of the "countess" (that's the name we gave her during our journey, so that's how I will refer to her), it was the nurse who came out to meet them. But they noticed that her name was not on their list. She was not their concern. They needed only that enemy of the people, the countess.

This was the first wave of deportations and no one knew where we were being taken, whether to prison or elsewhere. The "nurse" (this is how the countess referred to her, so I will too), tried to convince the soldiers that the countess was frail and ill, that there could be no possible reason for them to take her. But her arguments met a stone wall of indifference. She then declared that she would not let the old lady go alone and began packing things into the countess's old-fashioned black bags. It then dawned on the Red Army guards that she intended to go with her charge. At first they were completely dumbfounded and then they began to protest. But the nurse paid no attention at all to them. She began to dress the countess and prepare her for travel. A few telephone calls were made to the "powers that be" but the Red Army guards were in a hurry because dawn was breaking and they had to complete their "work" while it was still dark. They grew tired of trying to explain everything and so they took both women. Difficulties arose when they tried to move the countess as she was too feeble even to stand on her own. Finally, they seated her in the armchair and together with the weeping nurse took them, chair and all, to the station. Once again they asked the nurse, if she really intended to go. She confirmed that she did. "Well, if you want to—then to hell with you!" they said and with a rumble they slammed the door shut.

All day the elderly woman sat in her armchair, but some arrangement had to be made for her to rest at night. My mother decided not to use the pallet we had made for her from the wicker trunk and the smaller bundles. She insisted that the old invalid needed some sort of "bed" more than she herself did. And so my mother spent the entire three week trip in a sitting position while the old countess either sat in her armchair or lay on our basket. Toward the end of our journey she almost never rose.

She was not only physically ill. Apparently she had been housebound for quite some time. She had grown accustomed to the confined space of her room, to its familiar objects, to the same people, the same habits, the same atmosphere, and the same way of life, settled now for years. Suddenly finding herself in a boxcar, amid a crowd of strangers, and under the most primitive circumstances it was not surprising that her state of mind became unbalanced. Perhaps at first, she was aware of her unusual surroundings, but soon everything became jumbled in her aged brain. The present and the past became entwined and fused into one. Her only link to reality was the nurse. The countess was sufficiently aware to know that we were all going somewhere by train and she kept giving the nurse such pathetically comic instructions as, "Be sure to reserve two hotel rooms," or "Hire a porter, don't carry the bags yourself, they're heavy..."

Whenever we managed to read the name of a station that we passed along the way, and the name would reach her ears, the countess would ask who owned this village. Sometimes she would supply the name herself.

"Oh yes," she would say, "This belongs to the Liubomirsky family," or "This group of villages belongs to the Vesolovskys. I've been here!" And then she would recall the names and events—the balls, the weddings, the funerals—that had brought her there.

The nurse sometimes became a bit impatient, sometimes a bit embarrassed by the elderly woman's incoherence. At first she attempted to explain our predicament to her. Then she gave up. She must have come to the conclusion that a clear sense of reality wouldn't be helpful to the countess anyway.

The train remained slightly longer in Kyiv. The countess demanded from the nurse that they disembark. She had been here before. She knew that it was a lovely city. She recalled some hotels where they could stay. She did not want to travel any further.

In her mind, of course, this was pre-Revolutionary Kyiv. From her comments it was apparent that she had once lived in this part of Ukraine and her married name testified to her husband's Ukrainian ancestry. The countess' semi-coherent speech, her confusion of the past with the dark present of the crowded boxcar, lent her words a curiously tragic, surreal quality.

Days passed. The countess became increasingly weaker. Lying on the hard basket, her thin frail body developed bed sores. Very little water was available. We were allowed, occasionally, to draw water from wells at the train stations, but the small bottles and pots which we used were hardly adequate containers for drinking water, much less so for washing. So the old body of the poor lady began to waste away. Each time we lifted her, the smell of her festering wounds filled the boxcar.

Then we had to clear the way to the little window, to open it and let in some fresh air.

The poor old dear began to ask, with increasing regularity, to be lifted. With childlike cunning, she would announce that she needed "to go." Then the nurse, with someone's help (frequently, my brother's), would seat her on the toilet which we had improvised from a chair, More often than not, the need turned out to be a false alarm. Then they would carry her back to her "bed." More and more, she wanted to make this trip from trunk to toilet and then back again. At the same time it seemed as if she was growing increasingly heavier, and the task became more and more difficult. Primarily it was because the nurse herself was losing strength. Only her kindness and gentleness never waned.

This nurse! Of uncertain age, dressed in her simple dark frock, she was neither pretty nor homely. So many of the people who underwent this difficult journey with us have faded from my memory; I could say very little, or perhaps even nothing at all about them. But this nurse is certain to have been remembered by all who were there. She was a symbol, a visible sign of the compassion and self-sacrifice of which humanity, writ large, is capable.

Just the fact that she was making this trip voluntarily made her remarkable. She was, after all, traveling with someone who was merely her employer, not a relative for whom such self-sacrifice might have seemed more natural.

I can still see her. Always there, next to the wicker trunk on which the old lady lay, seated in the armchair, her eyes focused on the countess, her hand holding her patient's tiny withered hand. She would rise only to prepare her patient's food or to rearrange her pallet. As soon as the countess felt the nurse's hand missing, she would begin to search restlessly along the surface of the covers as if for a lost treasure. If the search became in the least bit prolonged, she would call out in her feeble little voice, "Nurse....nurse..."

The nurse hardly had time to take care of her own bodily needs. Whenever she would go to our improvised and curtained-off privy, the frantic frail voice would call out to her.

All this continued—not for a day or two—but for almost three weeks. During this time, the nurse did not sleep. Sometimes, she might doze off, her head resting on the corner of the cot, but even these short naps would be interrupted by the old lady's, "Nurse...nurse..."

We all slept very little. Only the children had room to stretch out. However, regardless of the time, we could always see the nurse beside her patient, either rearranging something, or talking to her, and reassuring her like a child. Once, toward the end of the trip, we persuaded the nurse to lie down and rest. Someone had given up his own berth to take her place by the old lady. No more than five minutes passed before she rose again, distressed by the sound of the countess's voice, and returned to her accustomed spot.

Time passed. Locked in the boxcar as we were, we grew curious about one another. The persona of the nurse attracted the most attention by all. Off in their corners people speculated about the nurse's motivation to accompany the countess voluntarily. You could write several novels— or at least a few short stories—based on these speculations. Someone claimed that it was love for the countess's son that inspired such self-sacrifice on the part of the nurse. She had promised him that she would care for his mother, that she would never leave her. Supposedly, this was substantiated by nurse herself, because she once referred to the son not by his given name but as "he" and how worried "he" would be when "he" learned that his mother had been deported.

One day, by now deep in the heart of Asia, the guards called in a doctor who decided that the old lady needed to be removed from the train and taken to a care facility. The nurse demanded that she be taken off along with the countess, because she would not allow her to be taken alone. But, although the nurse was traveling voluntarily, she was not allowed to leave. Both remained on the train and traveled on. This seemed to further substantiate the romantic versions of nurse's self-sacrifice.

There were other versions, too: the nurse was the countess' illegitimate daughter, or maybe the illegitimate daughter of someone in her immediate family. Or it was because of the countess's wealth and the nurse's desire to inherit it.

For a while, a young man, the son of a Lviv banker who was traveling with us, volunteered to help with lifting the invalid. He often sat next to the nurse and carried on whispered conversations with her. The nurse was our neighbor in the boxcar and my brother frequently helped her so she grew to trust us. She told us that this enterprising young man tried to find out from her if perhaps the countess had not left behind some valuables in Lviv--- and just where she might have hidden them. He asked where she lived, whether she had any jewelry and how it was being safeguarded. All that—in the event he might make it back to Lviv.

These speculations, regardless of their nature, did not diminish the respect everyone felt for the nurse, although somehow it never occurred to anyone that her voluntary exile was inspired simply by a profound human kindness and loving concern for the helplessness of another human being.

After we arrived at our destination, a tiny railroad station in the middle of the steppe in that part of Kazakhstan that once was known as Sybkrai, wagons—drawn by horses and oxen—as well as trucks pulled up to the railroad cars. The countess was placed into her armchair and then armchair and all, she was lifted onto a horse-drawn wagon. The nurse wept as she said farewell to us. Then her tragic caravan departed. We were taken to a different settlement.

Sometime that autumn, the nurse came to see us, wearing the same simple dress and a little beret. Tearfully she related that soon after being brought to a collective farm far out in the steppe, the countess had died. The nurse tried to obtain a permit to return to Lviv. No one wanted to hear her explanation that she had come here voluntarily, so she decided to go home without permission.

Never had anyone, who tried to make their way back on their own, ever been successful in getting very far. But the nurse spoke good Russian, and it seemed that with her unassuming appearance she would not stand out among other Soviet travelers. So with her old-fashioned bag in hand, she left. We lost track of her for a brief time. But, after several weeks, we received news that she had been caught and was returned to Kazakhstan—this time to prison.

After amnesty was declared, the nurse was released and we again had occasion to meet. She told us how, alternately hitching rides in cars, traveling by rail, and walking, she had trekked with a similarly unfortunate woman all the way back to Ukraine.

Upon reaching Ukraine, they went from village to village, gradually making their way westward. Along the way they met people who, even though in fear for themselves, were nonetheless willing to provide them with as much food as they could spare and directed them to the best roads to follow. They got as far as the river Zbruch. Finally, one dark night, as guards closed in on her from both sides of the bridge, she had no more strength left to flee and so, sitting there, on her old fashioned bag, she was caught. Her explanation, that she had gone to Kazakhstan voluntarily, was ignored. She was convicted of unlawful flight.

Those who spent time with her in prison recounted that she was always willing to help others, even at the expense of her own needs. She frequently spoke of her old countess for whom she cared for so many years and who died in her arms.

I always recall the nurse whenever human egoism, selfishness, greed and malice seem to deny even the very possibility that there may actually exist a genuine human being writ large.

Chapter 4:

Akhmir

Slowly our convoy of ox-driven wagons moved away from the train station and out into the Kazakh steppe.

The fact that the doors of the confining boxcar had been unlocked and we could exit gave us, at first, a sense of liberation. The openness, the crisp fresh air—this seemed like freedom. But we quickly realized that the boundless open space before us might as well be a barbed wire fence. There was no crossing it and there would be no road home for us.

In places, the steppe was still covered with snow, though slushy now and no longer very white. A bitterly cold wind and the blowing sand seemed to impede even the slow but sturdy oxen. They trudged on, their heavy heads moving in time to every step. The wagons creaked and bounced on the uneven steppe road.

After nearly three weeks in the stuffy boxcar, the fresh air was intoxicating. In a stupor, we sat atop the wagons muffled in every way possible, first warmed by the sun and then frozen by the wind.

The deportees were seated on the wagons and the guards who also served as teamsters walked alongside, occasionally hopping on the wagons to sit for a while. There were five: three "*khakhlushky*"[2] and

---

2   *khakhol* (Russ., m.) A demeaning colloquial term used by Russians against Ukrainians; *khakhlushky* is the feminine plural form.

two Kazakhs. One of the Kazakhs, Askar Ablkaz, was the head of the *kolhosp*—the collective farm—in Karhala. The other Kazakh, the older one and the herdsman at the farm, was Akhmir.

Akhmir's inverted fur-lined trousers, stuffed into his heavy felt boots made his legs appear inordinately bowed. He also wore a quilted jacket and a cap with earflaps, but his cap was different from the ones we had seen worn by Russians. It reminded us of drawings of Genghis Khan's warriors. The cap rose in a tall sharply rounded cone and it was trimmed all around with fox fur. The fur trim was widest above the forehead and fell in the back in graceful waves. On both sides of his face, the fur earflaps hung all the way down to the shoulders. Since Kazakhs never tied them under their chins, the earflaps rose and fell to the shoulders like wings whenever they walked quickly or rode their horses.

Dark squinty eyes over prominent cheekbones peered at us beneath the edge of the shapka. Akhmir had a sparse spiky beard that protruded slightly, a flat, wide nose, and a face burned by the sun, wind and frost.

Akhmir was not the captain of this convoy. The leader was Askar, who was clearly enthusiastic about everything "Russkoye." Even his shapka was not an old-fashioned one like Akhmir's but a plain Russian-style ushanka. He even spoke a little Russian.

We tried to get him to tell us where we were being taken and what we could expect to find there. But beyond enthusiastic assertions that things there would be "very good" we learned nothing. Askar's especially annoying assurance, "Never mind, you'll get used to it," sounded too much like "give ye up all hope." We had no intention of getting used to anything.

Askar was the head of the collective farm to which we were being taken. Some people tried to ingratiate themselves by presenting him with gifts. Perhaps they thought that, in the future, such gifts might lead to better job assignments at the *kolhosp*. Someone even gifted him with… a tuxedo. Later, on his day off, Askar paraded around the farm in it but, clearly, the gifting didn't have its desired effect.

My tiny hand mirror slipped out of my pocket and fell beneath the wagon. Askar caught it so eagerly that I decided to give it to him. At the next rest stop, my mother signaled to me with a silent nod toward something under the wagon. I could barely restrain my laughter. The chairman of the collective farm was lying there, on the damp ground, on his back, holding my mirror to his face. He was gazing at himself admiringly, making faces, furrowing his brow, and baring his teeth.

Although Askar was the captain of the convoy, in the evenings when we stopped to encamp, it was Akhmir who went into action. It was he who picked out the camp site—as sheltered as possible and near water. And it was he who started the fire using dried cow dung which he and the girls had gathered from the steppe. Even with all my scouting experience I was at a loss to explain how it was possible to light a fire using such soggy fuel. Of course, this was not some huge bonfire; it was just a tiny campfire. Nevertheless, we all huddled near it just to warm ourselves a bit, because immediately after sunset the steppe would become so cold that it—and even we—would be covered with white rime blossoms. Those who owned cook pots put them onto the coals of the dung-fire to boil water.

For four days our ox-drawn convoy continued in this way across the treeless steppe. We were alternately frozen by the wind and burned by the sun. Some were burned so severely that their faces swelled.

Now and then we would come across a settlement—consisting of a few gray houses with flat roofs, distinguishable from the steppe only when we came near. So when something appeared on the horizon that seemed to be a stand of trees, we were incredulous. Maybe this was only an illusion—a mirage? But no, we drew nearer and it was still there. These were trees! Not only trees, but trees by a river! Our convoy gradually approached them and we made camp along the river bank.

It was now the month of May—the beginning of Siberian spring. The ice on the river had already begun to thaw but it had not melted completely. A large block of ice floated down the river. In some places the river seemed to be covered with a gruel of mushy ice. This spot was a river ford and in the summer it was so dry that it was quite possible to wade across without wetting one's knees. Now, however, the river had a fierce appearance and it spread its turbulent and muddy waters far and wide.

As soon as we came close to the river, Askar became ill. He groaned, clutching his head dramatically and repeating in Kazakh, "Bas auruda, [my head hurts]". Finally he became so weak that he needed to lie down in one of the wagons. There he stayed until we reached the river.

Encamped on the other side were other deportees, like us. They had arrived here two days earlier in their horse-drawn wagons. We shouted across the river. They promised to send some food in exchange for clothing. A boy on horseback carried the food across the river. We watched anxiously as the horse battled the current amid the blocks of ice and the icy gruel. He brought over bread and eggs. Then there was more cross-river trading.

Akhmir lit a fire on the river bank and so we passed the night. In the morning the wagons lined up and began their river crossing. When the first wagon, driven by one of the girls, reached midstream the oxen panicked and refused to proceed any further. A large block of ice floated by and the wagon began to tilt. The deportees' precious bundles of belongings began to spill into the frigid water, onto the chunks of ice and into the icy slush. Beyond the bundles, we saw as one of the deportees—who suffered from tuberculosis—began to slide. He was on the verge of falling in.

On the bank Akhmir and Askar exchanged harsh words in Kazakh, unintelligible to us. Askar kept pointing at his head and moaning. It was no use. Akhmir rolled up his fur-lined trousers and waded into the river. With his help the wagon was righted and reached the other side. In the same way, Akhmir guided the other wagons across. There, a fire was built to dry out the wet clothing and belongings. We wrapped the sick man, who had fallen into the river, in dry blankets.

As we started out again, Askar began to recover. Now he moaned only a little. We passed through a village where the deportees whom we had gotten to know at the river crossing stayed behind. Once we left that village Askar was completely restored to health.

On the evening of the fifth and final day of our oxcart journey we came to another stand of trees. We were told that this was the village of Karhaly, the *kolhosp* to which we had been assigned. Our convoy paused momentarily. The wagon line-up was rearranged. We surmised that this was the result of the discussion between Askar and Akhmir. It was a concession from Askar in exchange for his "illness of convenience" by the river. Now the oxcart on which Akhmir was seated led the convoy. All other wagons fell in behind.

It had become a pleasant day. Even the wind died down. We rode into Karhaly. There was only one, very wide and grassy street. Flat-roofed houses made of sun-baked brick, stood on either side. They were turned sideways, with not a single window facing the street. Here and there trees grew between the houses. People lined the street. They had come out to greet, or perhaps just to take a look at those people that they had been told about--- those capitalistic bloodsuckers.

Akhmir, proudly erect on his wagon, rode in first. His Mongolian ancestors must have ridden in similar fashion, when bringing captives from a distant military campaign. Those slaves, taken by Akhmir's ancestors, must have felt the same way as we did now.

In the very middle of the street at the entrance to the village, the figure of a little boy appeared. The child ran forward to meet the wagon, thrusting his joined hands into the air. Akhmir scooped them up into his own large hand, and in one motion he lifted the child up high and seated the boy beside him. And so the two of them, grandfather Akhmir and his grandson Urusbai, rode triumphantly into the village. Proud, and I think happy, but unaware of the despair that overwhelmed those they brought with them.

After being settled at the collective farm we were immediately driven out to work in the field. This was spring and the fields had to be sown quickly. That's why "skilled" workers—such as we—were so necessary.

We then learned that the young boy was Akhmir's grandson. His father had committed suicide. According to Kazakh custom Akhmir's second son, Mamerbai, should have married the widow. But he did not want to marry her. Maybe it was because she herself was the cause of her husband's death or maybe it was because he was young and had no desire to comply with old customs. He did, however, take it upon himself to raise his nephew. Because Mamerbai, like Askar, was enthralled with all things Russian, he named the boy Urusbai. "*Urus*", in Kazakh means "Russian" and "*Bai*" means "master." Nonetheless, it was mostly the boy's grandfather Akhmir who cared for the boy and he was raising him traditionally. For them both, the steppe and horses were the very essence of life.

Akhmir's attitude towards us was one of indifference. During our trek, he seemed to regard us like so much livestock, merely laborers that had to be delivered to the village. Little Urusbai was a little afraid of us, as is every child of strangers. But he was also curious. Sometimes, in his childlike way, he would tease us. He would come running around the corner and swat my arm with his plump little hand. When I once caught his hand in mine, he struggled desperately and tried to break away like a little trapped animal until I let him go. With time I taught him how to play "peek-a-boo" so that whenever he would see me, he would shout "peek-a-boo!" from afar. Perhaps it was only then that old Akhmir began to regard us as humans. The fact that we played with and entertained his beloved grandson placed us within his circle of friends. But Mamerbai was not pleased that the child had contacts with the political deportees.

Everyday, when we would return from the fields, half-dead with exhaustion, we could see little Urusbai walking in the middle of the wide street. Kazakh children look like little Buddhas. The round plumpness of their faces softens the sharpness of their cheekbones. The slant of their dark eyes lend further charm. Little Urusbai also had that endearing smile of a merry mischief-maker. His tiny figure seemed even smaller in the middle of that immensely wide street. He strode proudly, happily and "importantly," because his grandfather Akhmir was riding in on horseback from the steppe, followed by a whole herd of *kolhosp* cows with a huge bull at its head. Urusbai would approach the horse, thrusting his clasped hands upward, until Akhmir, in one motion, lifted him and seated him in front of his horse. Together in this way they rode through village.

The sky, completely cloudless throughout the day, would suddenly gather clouds in the evening. Amidst their rolling golden curls the setting sun would bathe the silhouettes of riders and the dust cloud of the herd in a crimson light. The air would be suffused with the scent of wormwood, the pungent smell of cattle, and the smoke of burning *karahainyk* wood and *kiziak* dung patties coming from the chimneys. In warm weather the riders would wear their little flat caps—*tiubitiyky*. During the cold season, the winged fox fur earflaps of their *shapky* would dance in time to the gait of their horses. There was something very primeval in the appearance of these Kazakh ponies that moved in their characteristically lurching gait and in these horsemen who rode with their feet stuck out in accompaniment to the sound of hoofs and the lowing of cattle. It made it easy to imagine that this was not the twentieth century at all, but some distant past when a simple—perhaps—but free and proud Kazakh nation roamed the Kazakh steppes.

Chapter 5:
Our Horse Adventures

For most people an aquamarine is a semi-precious sparkling greenish gem, but for me the word always conjures up a noble thoroughbred horse. To be perfectly honest, I only knew this horse from a photograph that had been in our home as long as I could remember. The photo was one of Aquamarine standing there with his head held high, and, of my father, seated atop him, wearing the uniform of a *strilets*[3]. In the picture, my father is holding the reins in his hands, smiling and looking off into the distance. Father often spoke about this horse with deep affection, as if it were a human and not a horse.

For me, of course, my father was always a dignified gentleman, his black hair prematurely silvered at the temples, always gentle, always composed and deliberate in his actions. But Father as astride Aquamarine—well, that was another Father altogether; this one had the romantic aura of a cavalry rifleman about him, riding out boldly, fighting for life and liberty. And actually, I think that was how he preferred to think of himself. But as long as I remembered him, he was no longer sitting on a horse in a military uniform; instead he was clad in lawyer's robes, standing in court before a judge and jury, and fighting for the life and liberty of his political-prisoner clients.

---

3   *Strilets*: a cavalry rifleman of the Sichovi Striltsi (1917-1919), a regular military unit in the Army of the Ukrainian National Republic

I think it was Aquamarine who infected all of us children with a love for horses, though—for us city kids—that love was to remain mostly, but not always, platonic.

First of all, there were real horses in Pidliute. For many of us just hearing the name "Pidliute" quickened our hearts and elicited pangs of longing. But for those for whom it may be just a geographic designation, let me explain: Pidliute is a village situated on the icy and brisk Limnytsia River deep in the wild Gorgany range of the Carpathians. Located just a bit below that village, following Limnytsia's run, was the famous *Plast*[4] camp, Sokil for older scouts and Ostodor for younger scouts. Further up the mountain was "Osmoloda," where the engineers and other employees of the metropolitan-archdiocesan forest estates lived. The Metropolitan Archbishop at the time was Metropolitan Andrey Sheptytsky.[5] And it was to Pidliute, with its healing mineral waters, where we would go for our annual vacations. Each Saturday gentlemen-engineers would arrive there too, frequently on horseback. Tying up their horses at the hitching posts outside the pavilion, they would go in to play bridge or to bowl. What they chose to do for their entertainment wasn't at all important to us; what was important was that we were allowed to ride their horses while they were inside. These rides, of course, were not free of mishaps.

My father always enjoyed telling the story of when he saw me riding horseback for the first time. As I rode behind a huge haystack, my mount and I disappeared from view. By the time the horse reappeared on the other side of the stack, he was riderless and happily grazing. What had happened was that he had walked right under an apple tree where its branches plucked me up into their bowers and then dropped me onto the ground.

One time my girlfriend, the beautiful Kuka, rode a horse out onto the main road, where the horse immediately set out in the direction of his own stable, that is, toward Osmoloda. Kuka had no idea how to turn him around and it was only by the time she was halfway there that she was able to stop him; she slid off his back and, holding on to the reins, she led him to a rail fence. Here she climbed over to the other side, at a safe distance from the horse, and tearfully waited until a passing

---

4   *Plast*: the Ukrainian Scouting Organization
5   Metropolitan Andrey Sheptytsky was the most revered and influential figure of the Ukrainian Greco-Catholic Church of the twentieth century.

Boyko[6] peasant came to help her. He turned the horse around, all the while bitterly muttering something about spoiled children who think they know how to ride. He then helped Kuka up into the saddle and pointed the horse back to Pidliute.

Sometimes a horse-drawn wagon, belonging to the scout camp would come through the village. It was on its way to pick up bread from Osmoloda. We would all run out to look, especially because it was always driven by an older boy scout, frequently a *lisoviy chort*.[7] The girls always tried to "just happen" to be standing along the road. Sometimes, on the return trip, with the wagon fully loaded, we had to help push the wagon. The poor unfortunate nag of a horse hardly seemed able to stand on its own. As the property of some uncaring peasant, it had almost starved to death before being rescued by the scouts. It seemed to me that only scouts could love such a creature and treat it with care and tenderness.

But my real horseback riding didn't actually begin until I visited a friend in Yanchyna where they bred and kept horses. And what horses these were! How wonderful it felt to leave the estate grounds and ride out onto the thoroughfare in a borrowed pair of riding breeches and hat with its obligatory feather. What a feeling that was—when I'd finally fall into the rhythm of the horse's gait, and yielding to that rhythm I'd experience an exhilarating unity of horse and rider! And then, with my heart pounding, I'd bring the horse to a gallop, racing along paths that border the grain fields—the pride of the distinguished owner of Yanchyna—up to the top of the hill from which I'd take in the knolls, the slopes and the fields. The wind blowing in my face and smoothing the grain-sown fields, I'd fly faster and faster among them, leaving a dusty cloud in the road behind me.

Those were our idyllic times with horses; later it was different.

They deported us to Kazakhstan. We were brought to a *kolhosp* on a Sunday afternoon; by noon on Monday they led us out into the fields to show us where we would be assigned to work. Why I was chosen from among all the deportees, I don't know. Suffice it to say that they took me out to the tillage area, showed me a troika of horses harnessed to a

6   Boyko: a native of the highland region of Boykivshchyna
7   lisoviy chort: a member of the Ukrainian scouting fraternities *lisovi chorty* ("Forest Devils")

harrow and told me to start cultivating the soil. I was supposed to follow a girl who, I later learned, was known as *Komsomolka*[8] Katia.

Well, a horse is a horse. I bravely walked up to my troika and, imitating Katia, set off to work. First off, I had to get up on one of the end horses. Well, then the fun began! This was not going to be easy. The horse had neither saddle nor stirrups, only a halter. For me (not exactly a great gymnast) just climbing onto the horse's back was quite a feat. And then, once there, without a saddle, I had to keep myself from falling off his bare back!

After only a few steps it was obvious that my past experiences in horseback riding simply did not apply. I didn't know where I should focus my attention first. Was it to control the rebellious troika and keep it to the precise pattern set by the team of horses led by the girl ahead of me? Or was it to keep myself from sliding off the back of my horse and falling beneath the hooves of his neighbor and onto the sharp teeth of the harrow that bounced off the freshly cultivated clods of dirt, barely broken by the harrow ahead of me? The coarse, shaggy late-winter coat of the horse began to rub my legs which were bare, protected by neither pants nor boots. Very quickly red streaks appeared on my legs where the skin had abraded. In addition, the neighboring middle horse kept pressing my inside leg and each of the three horses wanted to go off in different directions.

More than anything else, now I desperately wanted only to stand firmly on the ground and on my own two feet. I wanted to be rid of these horses, of this growing sharp pain on my chafed legs and of everything else that was beyond my competence, my strength and my courage! But it was all impossible. Even if I could jump down from the horse onto the uneven clumps of earth, I would have been forced either under the horse's hooves or onto the path of the bristling teeth of the harrow.

As I thought about how I might dismount safely, my eyes focused on the troika ahead of mine. Katia was sitting on her horse, free and easy, as if in an armchair, effortlessly flipping both legs onto one side of the horse. Dangling her legs and letting them bounce off the horse's side, she would throw them over sometimes to the other side, and then like a circus performer she would leap from one horse to another. As

---

8   *komsomolka*: female member of *komsomol* the Union of Communist Youth

she jumped around, she'd shout at the horses in a wild voice, emitting hoarse and throaty sounds that were neither words nor simply noise. And then looking back at me... she laughed. No matter how often I looked up, tearing my gaze away from the heads of the horses that I tried to control, I always found her deeply tanned face with its prominent cheekbones and its row of white teeth grinning malevolently in my direction. Seeing that grin and those teeth, I knew: she was waiting for the moment when I would fall from my horse. My struggle with these horses was a terrific source of entertainment for her and she was just looking to see what would come of it!

Suddenly, unexpectedly, in an instant, I no longer felt any pain in my legs, which by this time were not only badly chafed but my muscles were cramping. In that moment I forgot about my fear of falling or having my leg crushed by the middle horse. Katia's laughter so stunned me at first that I completely lost control of the troika and nearly fell off my horse. But in one quick, if awkward, motion I crawled up onto his spine again and lay nearly flat on it. I tried to collect my thoughts which, slammed by a powerful emotion, suddenly seemed to have scattered in all directions.

In an instant everything else became secondary, altogether less important. I stopped wanting to land on my own feet, safe on hard ground—away from the horses, away from the harrow, away from all of this. Katia's laughter, her evil grinning, although at first seeming to paralyze me, forced me to focus all my strength on one task: I dare not fall, I dare not lose control over these horses, I must learn to master them. But first I had to overcome the pain of the abraded skin and my cramping muscles, for it was this very pain that kept me from taking control of the horses.

There were still many hours left until dusk and the end of the workday. I thought to myself, "I am undergoing a scout's trial of endurance." I remembered at the camp in Horyhliady and how it had been my turn to carry a water bucket which was far too heavy for me. I had marked out a goal for myself, a small distance that I would carry the bucket without resting. I would then increase the distance, until at last I forced myself to carry that full bucket for a very long way.

I applied the same method here. There—to that turn, then to the next one, just a little further, just a little further.

But more torment still awaited me. The harrow needed to be cleaned periodically. That meant that the horses had to be stopped when Katia stopped hers, I had to slide down, walk up to the harrow, lift it and then remove everything that had accumulated in its hooks. Earlier I had dreamt of finding myself on firm ground on my own two feet. Now my legs seemed to give way beneath me and I had to force myself to take those few steps to the harrow. And how heavy it was! Then back to the horses and somehow to climb back up again onto the horse's back.

I admit that the first time I had to ask Katia to help me, which she did, but with obvious malice. After this I tried never to ask her for anything again.

In the evening I slid off the horse and walked home. Actually, I didn't exactly walk but rather dragged myself, forcing myself to lift one foot after another. One more step, one more step.

But the day's woes weren't over for me yet. Mother was waiting for me at home. How was I to tell her that my legs were raw wounds, that every bone, every muscle felt crushed. Also, the other deportees wanted to learn what kind of work awaited them the next day, and I didn't want to frighten them. That would not be helpful for them tomorrow. But what could I do? It wasn't that I wanted to cry, the tears just rolled down my cheek by themselves. These weren't tears of self-pity, they were simply tears of pain. Only the memory of Katia's laughter slowed them somewhat and I managed to endure this trial of meeting with mother and the other deportees. Mother quickly guessed everything and to shield me from embarrassment, she hurriedly led me into the house and laid me on my pallet of straw.

The following day dug into my memory like a nightmare, like a series of unbearably painful moments strung together. Every movement of the horse generated a hundredfold pain and involuntary tears streamed down my face. And Katia always rode before me, bellowing inane ditties at the top of her lungs. I remember one of them:

> *"Shine on, you street lamp, shine on across ten-lines*
> *My sweetie is a komsomolets, but I am not a party member"*

Actually she was a *komsomolka*, and her mocking laughter forced me to find ways of mastering not only the horses but myself as well.

Despite the pain, on this second day I began to grasp the art of managing horses. Niura, the bookkeeper, rode up to me at one point. It was her responsibility to record just how much of the field each of us had plowed or tilled. For some time she rode beside me, observing the quality of my work; then she rode up to me and gave me a few hints to help me get the "tricks" of this work. Once she even cleaned the harrow for me, but before long she began to distance herself, because friendly contact with me would have incurred the displeasure of her fellow *komsomoltsi.*

In time, I learned how to keep myself atop the horse in such a way so as not to slide and how to change positions so as not to abrade my skin. At any rate, Katia, who still glared at me because my inexperience slowed work, stopped laughing at me, and sometimes, just in order to hurry the job along, she would clean my harrow on her own. After a few days they assigned me to a new job—with oxen. Although this was less "prestigious" work, I was happy to accept it. However, I was very afraid of the oxen and I honestly don't know which was worse, that fear or the hard labor and pain of working with the horses.

But our horse adventures did not end here.

Sometime during the middle of summer my brother was sent off to the neighboring village of Zharmy. He traveled there by wagon with other collective farm workers; maybe even the chairman of the *kolhosp* was with them. They left in the morning and were due to return that evening. Evening came and night fell and they still had not returned.

Our constant life companion in Kazakhstan was fear, fear of each approaching minute, fear of whatever the future may yet bring. As long as we were all together it was only half-bad. But whenever one of us was absent, then the anxiety, the waiting filled with apprehension, would begin. Because... who knew what could happen?

In total darkness, with no source of light, my mother and I sat outside the house and waited. Finally I persuaded Mother to go to bed, and I myself lay down but we both knew that there would be no sleeping for either of us. So there we lay in the dark, feeling each other's anxieties and fears.

We had prepared food for my brother and, on a metal tray (a remnant from home) we laid out twigs to be used as tiny torches to light the house since we had no lamps or candles. Everything was ready and waiting for his return. Only he was missing.

In the hush of the night, we listened to all kinds of sounds. Eventually we heard a wagon making its way down the middle of the road—it was the wagon which left for Zharmy in the morning. The wagon passed by, its sound gradually dying away. "Maybe they are all disembarking now and he will soon be here," we thought. But he did not come. I decided to go to the chairman of the *kolhosp* and find out what happened. I started to get dressed, but Mother stopped me. "It's dangerous to be walking alone at night. Let's wait a while."

Have you noticed how time has a way of stretching when you're waiting? Maybe it wasn't really so long, but for us it seemed like an eternity. At last I decided that I would go after all, and just then we heard a new sound in the night. It was the sound of hooves; they passed our house and then died away.

I was rising from my pallet when we heard some slow and heavy footsteps and finally my brother entered. He could barely walk and when we lit our "campfire" on the tray, we saw that his face appeared shrunken and dark. Yet it was so set and full of determination, that I held my tongue; I dared not ask him where he had been and what had happened.

Then he told us: they had gone to Zharmy to fetch a young unbroken stallion for the *kolhosp*. When they were given the horse, the farm workers placed a wooden Kazakh saddle on him and then proceeded to get into the wagon by themselves, ordering my brother to ride the horse back to the home village.

We have all seen broncos in films, so you know what it's like to ride such a horse. In addition, the Kazakh wooden saddle was adorned with metal studs, leather straps, thongs and God knows what else.

The *kolhosp* "potentates," seating themselves in the wagon, waited to see what would happen next. I was reminded of Katia watching me astride the troika horse when we were tilling the fields. Would he fall off or not? Would he take a tumble or not? The horse, naturally, began to act up immediately. One would think that after a few minutes of such a performance, they would have given up on the entertainment and simply led the horse to the wagon and tied him up to the back, or else they would have seated an experienced Kazakh herdsman atop him. But just as Katia and her ridicule affected me, so this audience, as it watched the horse leaping and jumping around and trying to throw and bite his rider, stiffened my brother's determination. He regained control over both the horse and over himself, and made the long ride back into our village. Although his legs bore the marks of the wooden saddle for quite some time, he nevertheless succeeded in arriving home alive and in one piece.

When we all finally lay down for the night, I still couldn't sleep. I remembered someone, long ago, telling me about an adventure my brother had had.

The date was July 1930. The *lisovi chorty* were holding a Grand Council near the village of Hadynia on the river Buh. Many of them (maybe twenty) had arrived; they were going to make a river trip to Polissia in three canoes.

They set up camp on the Buh river bank. Water—probably to make supper—was boiling in a cauldron over the campfire. Unexpectedly, two scouts on horseback arrived from a nearby parsonage. They joined the group as their horses grazed nearby. My brother decided that he wanted to go riding (he was probably tempted by the spirit of Aquamarine). He mounted one of the horses and began to ride along the river. The horse was not particularly docile but somehow they got along. When they neared the campfire the horse either stepped onto a branch that supported the boiling cauldron or he actually stepped directly into it. In any case, the boiling water spilled onto the horse. The scalded horse reared and took off down the wooded trail. My brother's scouting friends, among them my other brother, stood and watched in shock; they were expecting to see him fall off. But he didn't fall; holding fast, he quickly disappeared around the bend of the trail. The other rider jumped on his horse and began to chase after him. The two returned after a half hour and my brother (as I was told), still proudly seated in the saddle, pretended to be an expert in equestrian matters.

Maybe it was this episode that prepared him for his wild ride on the unbroken stallion in Kazakhstan. It could easily have ended in death or mutilation. Actually, I must admit, that deep down, I have always believed that it was the 'spirit of Aquamarine" that assisted us in our horse adventures.

Later, there would be different challenges. There was work with camels, and with oxen, with calves and even with *sarlyki* (animals similar to yaks). It certainly is easier to write about these experiences than to live through them!

Several years into our exile, I lived in a small house by a river at the very edge of the village. One time an acquaintance of ours, a deportee like ourselves, arrived from a neighboring village. They sent her in a little horse-drawn wagon. Hanusia unharnessed the horse, fettered him and let him graze. She herself went about her assigned chores. She asked me to unfetter him in a half hour after he had rested and then take him to the river so that he might drink.

I did everything as I was asked and in addition I looked out every few minutes to see if the horse was still there, to make sure he wasn't stolen—because failure to attend properly to horses carried a ten year prison sentence. When I looked out again, for who-knows-which-time, to check if the horse was still there—he was gone!

Despair enveloped me. The steppe is flat—you can see for miles. I started looking around. No horse. I climbed up on the flat roof of our house to look out in all directions. I could see people working in the fields on the other side of the river and beyond them the flat, open steppe with nothing on it. Without thinking about it too much, I tore down the road and went searching for him. I was certain that if he were not stolen by now he would have gone in the direction of "his" *kolhosp*—the horse ranch where they were housed and fed. So I ran in that direction.

Along the way I asked the fieldworkers. Yes, they had seen the lone horse, and they had wondered why he was running down the road alone.

I think this was the longest stretch I have ever run in my life and it was not to end soon. I do not know how far I ran and how far I walked when I finally glimpsed "my" horse as he ran out from behind a huge mound of hay and was being chased by a boy on another horse. My hope was that the boy might stop and capture the horse. This was not to be. Not only did he fail to catch him, he stole the bridle, as it later turned out. After a while my horse re-emerged from behind the hayrack heading toward his village. I followed him. Here, at least, I could see him. The river Char runs halfway between the two villages. I walked up to the river and waited. The horse had long ago made his way across the river and then disappeared from sight, hidden behind some willow trees growing along the bank. Somehow I needed to get to the other side.

Many rivers here dry up in the summer, but not all. This river Char was one of those exceptions. So where was the ford?

A Kazakh on a horse rode up. I began asking him if he might catch my horse for me—which is easy to do while riding. He seemed to agree, crossed the river but that was the end of it. It is true that I saw him urge his own horse in the direction of "my" horse, but before long he obviously grew bored, and as soon as my horse ran off, the Kazakh showed no further interest in chasing him and rode off in a different direction.

Standing on one side of the river I saw "my" horse calmly grazing on the other. How was I going to get to him?

Finally about a hundred meters away I spotted a place that could serve as a ford so I crossed the river there. "Just a little further," I thought "and I will have my horse." I watched him as he grazed. All I needed to do was to walk up to him and take hold of him. Even from afar I could see that his bridle was missing. How would I capture him?

"If I have to grab him by his mane, I will!" I thought.

I walked up to the horse and he, sensing something, ran off. So I became even more discreet, approaching him more slowly. I was really quite close.

Again I thought, "Just a little more and the horse is mine."

But no! I hadn't even come up halfway to him when he walked away from me. So even more cautiously, even more deliberately and ever so slowly I approached him from behind.

I thought, "When I'm really, really close I'll grab him from the side."

Forget it! Nothing worked!

As if that wasn't enough, it seemed that the horse was beginning to make fun of me—or maybe he was playing a game. When I first began my pursuit of him, he would run away from me when I was still twenty or thirty meters away, now he'd let me come as near as a few meters, grazing calmly until the very last moment. And then, when I was very close to him, thinking that he hadn't noticed me at all, he'd turn around and, looking directly at me with his shining dark eyes, he'd wait. As soon as I was next to him--- he'd jump away and run off in an unexpected direction where again he'd begin to munch on the grass. Throughout all of this, he never deviated from the direction back to his ranch.

I tried devising new tactics. But no matter how clever a method I attempted, the horse was always more clever and faster than I.

This went on for I don't know how many hours. And throughout this game of tag we kept drawing nearer to the ranch. I could see from afar a herd of horses grazing in the steppe along with its Kazakh herdsman on horseback. As soon as my horse sighted the herd he picked up his pace and quickly disappeared from sight.

I walked up to the herd and began asking the herder to catch my horse for me.

"Oh yes," said the herder, "I saw him here, he has already joined the herd. But it won't be possible to catch him. He's the kind of horse that can't be caught out on the steppe. If you want to harness him, you need to do it while he's still in the stable. When I drive the herd back to the farm, then we'll catch him."

This information soothed my ego somewhat, but it really didn't help my situation one bit. I returned empty-handed to my village. Midway home I met Hanusia. When she had returned to the house after work and saw only the wagon there, she guessed what had happened and decided to follow me in looking for the horse. Now she had to walk back to the ranch and ride back again tomorrow to return the wagon.

Once home I calculated that I had traveled twelve kilometers chasing "my-not- my" horse back to his ranch—and this doesn't take into account all the turns I had to make when the horse was playing games with me! I had traveled that distance, partly walking and partly running. Then, I had to double that figure again for the trip home. Even more than the fatigue, what bothered me most was worry about the difficulties that Hanusia was bound to encounter back at the farm—not only because of the runaway horse, but also because of the missing bridle. After some questions and hints I figured out who it was who had stolen the bridle. The boy refused to return it, although I went pleading for it to his parents. The bridle was gone. As repayment we had to work off additional hours.

And so it is with these horses which we love so much. They bring us so much suffering and worry. But don't think for a minute that I will ever stop loving them!

Chapter 6:

O My Oxen...
My Curley-horned Oxen!

It was still dark and it seemed to me that I had just gone to sleep when the sound of horse's hooves reverberated outside our window. The work brigade leader was using the crop of his whip to knock on our small window, all the while shouting at the top of his lungs, "Uliana, Uliana, *haida, haida*—hurry up, hurry up!"

After bellowing like that, he lashed his horse and rode off. He went this same way from house to house, gathering all the members of his brigade for work in the field.

There probably were worse, more painful, and more humiliating moments and experiences than this but I have to admit that this call aroused such a rage in me that I wanted nothing more than to strike out at the hapless brigadier with my fists. I think my fury came less from the fact that I was dead tired from the previous day's work, than from the nightmarish reality of our serfdom—represented by that horse at our window, that brigadier's whip knocking on it, and that detested *haida, haida*!

But my anger would find no relief (unless it was an occasional tear—hidden, so as not to alarm Mother), because the brigadier rode off at once, together with his "*haida, haida,*" and we had to get up and go to the fields.

Feeling our way around in the dark (because we had no indoor source of light until later that autumn when we first received candles from Lviv—and then, much later, a small kerosene lamp) we dressed and went into the village. Emerging from their houses, dark silhouettes of people gradually appeared and then headed out into the steppe.

I suppose I should have enjoyed walking out in the predawn twilight among the blooming bushes of the *karahainyk* and the spring fragrances that blew from the steppe. It was impossible not to succumb to the charms of nature—even here! But at some subconscious level I could not fully rid myself of my internal anxieties and apprehensions about my immediate future.

About a kilometer or more beyond the village, in a meadow by the river, which the summer sun had not yet dried up, there was a herd of oxen grazing. We left them there after the previous day's work. Now it was my task to find, rope, and harness to a harrow the pair of oxen that had been assigned to me from among this herd. One of the oxen was called Maiboroda; the other had no name, only a number—18. I think as long as I live, I will never forget that number. Frankly, I always felt that it wasn't the oxen who had been assigned to me, but rather that somehow *I* had been yoked to them. Their numbers were branded on their horns.

The very sight of this herd that had moved out into the steppe overnight but still somehow kept itself together, filled me with fear. Such a mass of lowered heads and branching horns! And now I had to walk into this herd and then, either avoiding or leaning on their strong and heavy bodies and their horned heads, I had to find my Maiboroda somewhere in this dense mass. The other, no-name ox was usually nearby because, working in pairs, they had become used to one another.

It may seem silly to some, but I have to admit that my heart was in my throat and despite the morning chill I was drenched in a nervous sweat. I kept slowing my pace, hoping to delay the moment when I would actually have to approach the herd. The moment arrived nonetheless. I wished (oh how I dearly wished!) that I could just simply close my eyes as women do when they're afraid. But, obviously, no one can walk into a herd of oxen with their eyes closed! I had to master my fear.

In time I worked out a system of ways of overcoming my fear, or at least its symptoms. But back then I wasn't able to deal with it very well. In my imagination these oxen kept doubling and tripling. How in the world was I supposed to control them? Maiboroda, of course, sensed my fear very well, as all animals do. He would graze peacefully until the moment that I approached. As soon as I'd try to come upon him unnoticed and attempt to place the rope around his horns he would shake his heavy head and taking a few quick steps, move off aside into a crowd of other oxen.

Nearly everyone else had already captured their oxen, so my two had even more room to run away from me. Occasionally an experienced kolhosp worker helped me hold Maiboroda down by the horns (curiously, an ox, as soon as he feels a firm hand upon him, relaxes). But that only happened when those with whom I was assigned to work grew tired of waiting. Time was passing, and we all had quotas to fill. Also, working in the morning was easier—the sun was not as hot. So everyone needed to hurry.

Finally my Maiboroda and Number 18 were caught. I held the thick rope in my not-too-powerful hand, the other end was wrapped around their horns, and I led (or rather pulled) them to the harrow, all the while shouting *haida, haida* and *tsob-tsob-tsabeh*, like the brigade leader who bellowed at me in the morning. The harrow was waiting for me near the field that would be tilled that day. Then the last thing left for me to do was to place the yoke on them, lock it in with a pin and finally begin my long day's work.

At that moment I felt a little relieved, because, yoked, somehow these beasts were not so fearsome. On the other hand it also signaled the start of the torturous workday. Walking over the freshly plowed soil, still wet from recent snows, my feet would get mired in the muddy dirt, so sticky that it became very hard to lift them. There was no appropriate footwear available so I didn't know what to wear. The cold and prickly ground made it impossible to walk barefoot. I had to stop, over and over again, take off my shoes and scrape out the dirt that had oozed in. The muscles in my legs ached as they sank into the muddy earth. My arms ached too, because the oxen had to be led by pulling on the rope.

By the time we'd finish harnessing the oxen, it would be dawn and up in the sky our friend—the meadowlark—would appear. He'd soar into the sky and, there, pour out his trilled song. Whenever I was overwhelmed, I would lift my head, look up and listen to the lark. Small yellow birds settled on the tracks of the recently tilled soil. I never did learn their names. Transforming the ground into a lovely yellow field, they followed the harrow and covered the black earth like shimmering flowers. Time and again, perhaps startled by our "tsob-tsabe," they would explode into the air only to fall to the ground again in a yellow carpet.

We were supposed to till the fields following a "two-track" method, that is, each field had to be harrowed first with one team and then immediately followed by another. If we worked alone, without the local people, we could speed our quota a bit by not doubling the tilling but by splaying it and harrowing side-by-side. Whenever we saw the distant outline of the brigadier on horseback, coming to check our work, the first one to sight him, would whistle and we would quickly rearrange ourselves into the prescribed two-track formation.

The fields varied, some were easier and some harder to work. The most difficult, but, of course, also the most beautiful, were the virgin fields. I vividly remember one field in particular.

The steppe was not perfectly flat in this one area. It was transected by a series of hills, unforested yet thickly but unevenly covered by *karahainyk* shrubs, spirea and some other prickly bushes whose leaves and blossoms reminded me of acacia. It was spring now and the shrubbery, the grasses and many, many wildflowers, some of which we had previously seen only as cultivated species in our gardens back home, were in full bloom here. Great splotches of yellow tulips, bearded anemones, all with their short-lived charm, marked off the boundary between the long winters and the torrid summers.

This virgin land had already been plowed. But heavy clumps of earth still held many shrub roots, and here and there among the clods a blooming branch of spirea would peek through. We had to break up the clods with our tillers and walk over them with our feet. The harrow skipped around, dragging the shrubs that had been scooped up along with the earth. Time and again it needed to be cleansed of everything that its iron teeth had trapped. Once, one of our workers cut his foot on the harrow, and a bloody stream from his perforated vein drenched the fat Siberian soil.

This new field had to be cultivated not only twice but three times. And all around this plowed area, an ocean of white blooming spirea bloomed. Our plowed strips were black islands amid this white sea. And rising high above us in the brilliantly blue sky was the meadowlark.

Towards evening, as it sometimes happened, gold-edged voluminous clouds would appear, seemingly from nowhere, there where the sun was setting. Our work was not yet done; we still had to finish tilling this plowed field that very day, so that we would not need to return to the same area tomorrow. Even after the moon came out against a darkened sky, we kept going round and round, dragging our oxen behind us.

Usually, towards evening the exhausted oxen gradually became more apathetic, more placid, so that even though they would plod along ever more slowly, they did not resist us. I liked to think that they sensed our fatigue and sympathized with us. But this one time their behavior was quite different somehow. Walking in one direction, they were generally unperturbed, but when we tried to turn them around, they began to shake their heads in an agitated fashion and tried to go back. Their normally sluggish movements became wilder and wilder and in a sudden twist of their heads my pair yanked the rope from my hand and swerving off to the side ran away. I was barely able to chase them down and it was only with great effort that I managed to redirect them to their designated course. But their erratic behavior didn't end, it continued after each turn.

After dusk the full moon, like a red ball, rose higher and higher and grew brighter and brighter. It gathered brilliance, casting ever more dense shadows as it did. Finally we understood. It was the magician-moon that affected our oxen so. As long as they were walking toward the moon, they were calm, but when we turned them around, and they saw their own horned shadows facing them, fear or perhaps some other anxiety overcame them, and they tried to turn back.

These yoked prisoners whom I feared so greatly were also awed by the moon, it seems—whether by its beauty or, perhaps, by some even more mysterious power.

Chapter 7:
Jok

A mongrel dog decided to attach himself to me. That red cur! For a tiny piece of bread he left his village and now he was trailing after me! I yelled at him, I tried to scare him away, I threw rocks at him. He would stop, stand motionless for a while and then he'd wag his tail and start following me again. Sometimes he'd run ahead of me and, lying in the middle of the road, with his head turned in my direction, he would wait for me.

I was returning from the *kolhosp* empty-handed—with no package, no letter, nothing but this pesky dog.

The day before, we had been informed that there was a package waiting for us at the post office. What joyous news! Perhaps there were letters, too! Maybe there was news of Father, maybe a letter for my brother from his wife about their young son. Maybe a letter for me—even if not the letter I most desired, still, a letter for me from home—from the city where home had been.

The post office was located in a neighboring village, more than a dozen kilometers away. I left early in the morning; by the time I arrived it was hot already. The air had become thick and shimmery on the road of this hilly region of the steppe. The *karahainyk* had finished blooming and the steppe faded into the light of the sun.

A group of other hopefuls like me was already standing outside the post office. There was no sign of the postmistress. Finally when she came, she glowered at us deportees, then, slamming the door, she went inside. She refused to let us in. After a short time, she reappeared—and then walked away. We continued waiting. Each of us had come from a different kolhosp and we compared living conditions.

The noonday sun beat down mercilessly and there was no shade anywhere. For a little while I went indoors, invited by people we knew from the transport train. They shared an *izba,* a large cabin, with its owners. It was a little cooler inside. A sick child was convulsing in a fever. I stayed briefly, but then returned to the post office in the hopes that the postmistress would come back. Sitting down next to a *karahainyk* bush, I decided to eat the bread that Mother packed for me for the road and that's when the dog attached himself to me. He looked like a cross between a greyhound and a red fox and his eyes and pointy muzzle followed my hand each time I brought the bread up to my mouth. He stared at me so intently that I couldn't stand it any longer and I finally threw him the tiniest of morsels. And now I couldn't get rid of him. As I sat there by the post office next to the *karahainyk* bush the dog was behind me the whole time. Whenever I got up, he got up.

I waited until evening. The postmistress came again twice, and each time it was the same story--- she would walk in, and then she would walk out. She didn't even want to talk to us. I finally left for home. The dog followed. What would my family say to me? They were expecting a package or a letter—and I came home with a dog!

We named the dog "Jok." In Kazakh the word means "there isn't any," and in fact there "wasn't any"—food—that we could give him.

Nonetheless Jok followed me everywhere, step for step, even when I went to work.

Our next job assignment was making cattle manure briquettes for fuel. In the middle of the *kolhosp* courtyard there was a huge mound of manure left over from the previous winter. Our job was to scatter it, but before we could, since the center was still frozen we had to break it up with our shovels. Then we had to spread it until it formed a huge knee-deep circle. Next we had to pour buckets of water over it while horses stirred it until it formed a thick fetid paste.

The dog kept his distance. He lay there waiting for me in the grass beyond the reach of the foul smell. If the wind happened to carry the stink of the ripe manure in his direction he would move and lie down elsewhere. I, on the other hand, had no way of avoiding it. I had to step right into the dung pile. Standing there in front of it I felt nauseous but I refused to make a spectacle of myself. So I sank first one foot, then another into the congealed clumps of dung mixed in with chopped straw and weeds. It was cold and prickly. The sharp straw and the dried weeds dug into my feet.

We were then shown what we were to do next. The manure had to be packed into wooden molds and then pressed down and leveled with our feet. Using the rope attached to each of the molds I hauled them away to an open area. Like the mud pies which we used to make when we were children these manure cakes waited to be baked by the sun.

A smelly layer of dung coated my legs. Indeed, all of me—my clothing, my hair, my face, everything—it seems, was saturated with the smell of manure.

Jok smelled this, so that when we walked home he kept a respectful distance. I waded into the roadside ditch. There was still some water left in the bottom of the ditch, and it rinsed some of the manure from my legs. Its muddy bottom felt like a poultice for my sore feet. They were like a sieve, full of holes, pricked by the straw, the dried weeds, and even occasional pieces of metal and glass embedded in the manure-paste. I went to the well to wash myself, trying to rinse off all traces of dung. Then Jok would venture a little closer—but still not too close because it was impossible to rid myself completely of the stench that seemed to have settled into every fold of my clothing. Perhaps with time I might have gotten used to it, but now whenever I had to step into that smelly mush, I had to force myself. First one foot, then the other....

The processed manure bricks dried in the sun. They would become the *kolhosp's* winter fuel.

We were then reassigned to another job and Jok followed me there too. Now we were making bricks using clay. These bricks, also sun-baked and known as *saman*, would become the building blocks used for the construction of houses, barns and other small structures.

Our work crew consisted entirely of political deportees. We tried to get the kolhosp management to give us a horse to mix the clay. Instead, they promised to pay us extra, but they lied.

It appeared that someone had already tried to make *saman* at this same site. There was a small stream near the clay pit and we directed the water toward the clay. But within just a few days it dried up and not even a trace remained. Evidently that was why our predecessors here gave up. The *kolhosp* authorities hadn't bothered to tell us about this. We were simply required to deliver our quota of the finished *saman*.

Where could we draw the necessary water? The only water available was at the bottom of an abandoned well-hole. My brother devised a way to get at that water. He and another man took turns standing at the rim of the hole, while holding onto the crossbeam of the well with one hand and holding a bucket with the other. They would dip the bucket down into the bottom of the well, fill it with water and then pass it up. We would then take the filled bucket from them, and in turn, hand them an empty bucket. Fifty buckets—and then the men would switch. In the meantime we would quickly pour the water down a wooden trough, woosh! There it flowed onto the prepared clay which would then be formed into bricks. It was necessary to pass the water rapidly so that it could form a stream, otherwise the water would just seep into the ground. Finally the formed bricks baked in the sun.

Jok was always nearby. He'd nap in the grass. Sometimes he'd disappear. Probably he was off hunting for food then. He certainly wasn't getting enough from us.

I was not involved with the production of *saman* for long, maybe only for a week. One day I got lightheaded and dizzy. Then a fever set in and I began to shake. Nevertheless I didn't want to leave the job; after all, we were being paid jointly for this work.

Already by mid-morning Jok was showing signs of uneasiness. He seemed to sense that something was wrong with me. By noon I could no longer stand on my feet. I started for home. Jok followed me.

On a pile of clay my fellow workers placed a ladder, which they had borrowed from the *kolhosp* and covered it with a piece of cloth stuffed with straw. This became my sickbed. A rash covered my body. No one knew what this illness this might be. This was central Asia, after all—smallpox was possible.

This was probably the first time in my life that I was so sick. I became delirious. The *kolhosp* disappeared. I was in a different place. I was in a different dimension, somewhere between that which was and that which yet may be.

Only one thing stayed real for me. It was the tree near our house; I could see it through our tiny window, its green crown bending and waving in the wind. Still, it was not the poplar that I had so laboriously cared for here. In my fever it became for me all the trees in Yezuyitsky Garden that had murmured to me ever since childhood. Or maybe, it was my very own ancestor-tree. In its leaves I saw the faces of those no longer with us. The faces, at times, would draw very near to me—and then, becoming very small, they would recede into the distance.

A cuckoo bird landed on the roof. It began to call. But for me it wasn't a cuckoo bird, it was the voice of someone calling me, summoning me to a place of no return.

And the tree kept murmuring, alternately approaching and receding.

When I temporarily regained consciousness I learned that my brother had gone looking for a doctor who could tell us what this disease might be. Finally, a deportee-doctor came, using the inspection of the village nursery as an official excuse to travel the twenty kilometers to see me. He diagnosed my illness as measles, usually a relatively mild childhood disease but in this case an extremely virulent form. Most likely, I was exposed to it at the home of that sick child, when I went to the post office. So—I brought two things home with me that day: my measles and Jok.

Oh Jok! Whenever I regained consciousness and with no one else at home, I would see Jok near my pallet gazing at me. As soon as anyone would come into the house, he would tuck his tail between his legs and run out. He was not allowed inside; he would certainly bring in fleas. So he would go outside, take his place beneath the window, leaving it only to go hunting. He learned how to unlatch the door and as soon as everyone was gone, he'd appear by my ladder-bed. Whenever I raved in delirium, he would whine in response and comfort me.

For many days I was aware only of the tree—and in it, of all those faces, so near to me and yet so far away. I spoke with the tree; with it I lamented what should have been done differently and what should be otherwise. The tree shared my worries, it accused me, it pitied me, and it scolded me. At night the tree would disappear and as I kept my poor exhausted family awake, fear, loneliness and dread of separation overcame me.

I heard heavy banging on the wall. I saw a deserted and half-demolished shed and a huge bull, the same one that roamed the village streets at night, entering it. Ramming his head against the wall, which gradually seemed to thin and slide apart, he snorted angrily at me.

At night I felt myself sinking and disappearing. I yearned to see my tree again. I could reconnect with the world then, even if it were a world in some other and unique dimension, even a world that lay somewhere between what had been and a premonition of what was yet to come—a world of loneliness.

With time my periods of consciousness increased. Then I always felt Jok's presence next to my ladder-cot. Sometimes he'd put his muzzle right onto the edge of my pallet. If I put my hand out he'd put his paw in it and rest his ruddy, pointy snout atop it. He'd sit there watching me. If keeping that position became uncomfortable for him, he would shift paws and continue sitting there—until someone entered the house. Then he would leave. I will always remember him this way. Of course, whether we will remain in his canine memory as well—that I don't know.

Deep in my heart a part of me wanted to keep Jok with us, another part told me to give him away to someone who could feed him. Jok went with my brother to the neighboring village. They spent their last night together on the flat roof of a house. In the morning my brother gave Jok away to a man whose dog had been eaten by the wolves the previous winter. They tied Jok down so that he would not run after my brother and come home to me.

Whenever I see a red mongrel dog I still feel Jok's paw in my hand and I see his little snout, just as when he, my companion in my delirium, stood guard beside my bed.

Chapter 8:

Letters

My helpless infant heart
Trails after you, after you...
* * *
The day dies slowly.
At night black yearning
Will grip my heart, for you... for you....

V. Bobinsky

Today I exchanged one of my dresses for a table. I wore that dress when we last walked together in Yezuyitsky Park; we walked in anger, arguing. (It seemed not so long ago that I played hopscotch on this same sidewalk, hopping around in my white socks, from one chalk-drawn square to another.) It was just the two of us walking. I had agreed to meet with someone and it seemed to me that it would be dishonorable of me not to go; it would be cowardly. He asked me not to go. In fact, he said, not going would be a sign of courage. We might have resolved our differences perhaps, but just then an acquaintance came up to us. This was a casual friend, an ordinary, pleasant enough person, but at that moment I felt I hated him. We were forced to part without a chance to say everything that needed to be said. Because maybe... maybe.

Then war broke out. I saw him only once later, out on the street with some other people. Even though I'm terrible at remembering dates, I can tell you precisely when it was that I last saw him, because the next day we were deported.

Now I was sitting at this table which I had bartered in exchange for my dress and I was going to write a letter. Actually, I had already written several drafts, but never sent them. I carried them around with me, reread them and then tore them up. Now it was the same story all over again. I wrote and I tore—even though paper was so very expensive here in Kazakhstan. I so dearly wanted to write the very best love letter in the whole world. But it is as impossible to speak of love as it is to speak of fragrance. You can write about it only by comparing it to something else.

Back then love smelled of wild thyme, of grasses, of summer and youth, of woody sap, of something moist and pungent wafting from the forest.

We sat together in the clearing, many of us, an entire company of gay young people; but he had arrived late, coming out of the resin-laden woods. It was then that I first saw him—in that clearing near Pechenizhyn. We welcomed him into our merry company, and there was room for him to sit beside me. We talked about something terribly important. Oh, how I wish I could remember what that was now, but I've forgotten. Back then he was, for me, just another member of that delightful group. Back then, the whole world was fascinating to me and I loved everybody and everything.

The girls were going to sleep on cushions spread out in the middle of the manse drawing room, side by side—because there were so many of us. The boys were supposed to sleep on the hay in the barn. Actually, no one slept very much because we talked on and on until late and rose early to party again. The two of us spent the time together, talking. He intended to stay for only one day but he remained for two, or maybe three. He even had to take off his shirt collar because it had become soiled. When he took me to meet his aunt in Kolomyia, she was highly displeased. She said, "What is wrong with young people these days, coming to visit without a shirt collar!" That struck me as very funny; at the same time I was very sad that he had to leave, because I felt that I still had so much more to tell him.

He wrote to me later. I would receive his letters at the *Collegium Minus*. I reread them hundreds of times and as I did, he endeared himself to me even more. I was always running out to see if another letter had arrived. Then he wrote, "To hell with the gods and their charity." Apparently this was how he interpreted my friendly letters. And then he stopped writing.

A year passed, maybe two. He was going abroad. He came to say goodbye. We met in my father's office with its books and armchairs. As I entered—he rose. He was so tall, so slim. His eyes—were they dark or hazel? I don't know. I felt that suddenly the earth's sphere was hurling through space out into the universe and carrying me along with it. It was a moment of revelation! Suddenly, that which is not given to everyone, that once-in-a lifetime, unrepeatable great something had come to me. But now—he was saying goodbye, he was leaving!

There was still that goodbye walk out to the beech forest on the outskirts of Lviv. It was early spring and for the first time in my life I saw, or perhaps it was the first time I noticed, the silver-gray beech trees and the latticework of their pale green leaves against the blue sky.

Then there was the train, with him in the window. Many other people were also there to see someone off, but I saw only him and his eyes—and I don't know whether they were hazel or dark. And I felt that for me there would be no tomorrow.

But there was a tomorrow. There was a week, and a year. Only, throughout it all, my heart was squeezed, tight as a fist.

So why should it be surprising, then, that after several years, when he returned, I acted so badly. I wanted to shine before him—but I was mute and shy. He mistook my awkwardness for feminine wiles. That was what led to the argument in Yezuyitskiy Park, our final conversation.

"Never let the sun set on your anger!" I understood those words—no, more than understand them—I lived them as we were being deported. Because by then, nothing could be rectified and nothing could be said that had been left unspoken.

And as we were being taken away, some despairing impulse led me to return all his letters to me via my faithful Olius'ka. I was convinced that this would be the "end of all ends."

After all, why should we drag someone along with us? His letters were, at least, a shadow of that which bound us together. I wanted them to be kept safe somewhere—those most wonderful letters in the whole world!

He once asked Oliuska if he could write to me here, in Kazakhstan. Oh how I yearned to have a word—at least a word—from him! How I regretted returning his letters! And yet—it was he, himself, who wrote, "To hell with the gods and their charity."

So that's why I kept writing—and never mailing my letters.

Time passed. Life's scenarios took me down unintended and unexpected paths. Sometimes when I reflect on it, I like to play the "what if" game. What if that casual acquaintance had not interrupted our conversation in Yezuyitskiy Park? What if I had decided not to keep that rendezvous? What if I had written the most perfect love letter to him from Kazakhstan?

Sometimes I think that maybe… maybe his letters to me were only a literary exercise. But to believe that would mean to deny love itself.

Maybe, he is still living, somewhere on this continent. Perhaps he will read this, but then maybe he will cut short his reading because there is nothing more unreal than an old love affair.

But maybe… maybe he still remembers the thyme and rosin-scented clearing near Pechenizhyn?

*   *   *   *

His letters to me were burned. He had to leave them behind at his home when the Germans came looking for him and so his cousin burned them. She told me so herself. Thus nothing, no trace, not even ashes, remains of our love.

Chapter 9:

Tychon Moiseievych

I can't remember his last name, but it really isn't important. They called him Tychon Moiseievych. He was the warehouse manager at the "Roads Department" where I had been hired.

My initial work assignment was provisional, only two weeks. During this time I needed to prove that I was capable of bookkeeping, and, of course, that I could do it in Russian. I knew only a little of both, and what I knew, I knew badly, but I desperately needed this job. Winter was approaching, we had no provisions and work in the roads district office guaranteed a ration of wheat.

Even without bread or potatoes it was possible to survive by milling the wheat on a coffee grinder in order to make kasha, or those Kazakh delicacies, *tolkan* or *kurmach*. Therefore, faced with the alternatives—a hungry winter or work in the district office—I summoned all my abilities, wits and intelligence so that this trial period might end successfully. It was simply a matter of survival.

I sat in my assigned place, like a mouse trapped under a broom, as my co-workers stared at me with undisguised curiosity. I pored over the columns in the ledger that I was supposed to fill with "professional" notations. It seemed to me that I had been given some sort of puzzle to solve. I was so absorbed in trying to decipher the purpose of the file notations that I became completely oblivious to the fact that I was being scrutinized as some kind of suspicious creature from that other, "capitalistic" world.

After a few days, it appeared that my mute presence came to be accepted since interest in me abated. Semi-audible comments were almost all silenced. Gradually the basic why's, where's, and what's of the various spaces in the ledger became clear to me; by the time the two weeks were over I knew (albeit without any great skill) how to properly place numbers in their appropriate checkerboard slots. It was only then that I, in turn, began to observe my co-workers stealthily.

The office group was international in make-up. The director was a Pole. Up to the time of the revolution he had been a horse groom on some estate; then he joined the Bolsheviks, and after completing his communist party education, he rose to the position of director in this distant Siberian land. He seemed to have some organizational abilities but his writing skills were weak. The only example of his writing that I ever saw was his signature. The senior bookkeeper was a Siberian-born Russian. His assistant was also a Siberian native, but an ethnic Bulgarian. There was a Tatar who was the technician, a Russian Engineer from Leningrad and then there was me. From time to time the stock manager would appear in the office; and this was, in fact, Tychon Moiseievych. He was tall, skinny and wiry. He had a small head with a hooknose, and a long neck with a prominent Adam's apple. Add thin reddish hair to these traits, and you have a very different image from that of a prototypical Ukrainian *kozak*.[9] But as it turns out—although not a *kozak*—he was nevertheless a Ukrainian whose family had long ago settled in Siberia. It took me some time to discover this. At first I came to know a very different side of Tychon.

From all the commentary that took place behind my back, the most venomous and malicious regarding Polish gentry came from Tychon Moiseievych. These barbs were directed at me, because in the minds of the locals, all those who had been deported from the western regions of Ukraine, were Polish gentry, who sucked blood from the working classes. In the course of filling out the personal information form about myself and during that first interview I told them that I wasn't a Pole at all but a Ukrainian. However, attempts to correct this inaccuracy—and

---

9   *Kozak:* a bold and manly image based on the 17th and 18th century horsemen of the Ukrainian steppe who were militarily and politically organized to battle Polish, Russian and Turkish oppressors.

to say that we were, in fact, typically working class or hard-working middle class—would have been useless.

Besides, it was an unwritten rule not to ask about the reasons for one's deportation or what anybody's occupation was back home. It was taken for granted that everyone lied anyway in order to present themselves in a "better"—that is, a more useful light. So naturally, my declaration that I was a Ukrainian was accepted as some misguided attempt to ease my situation.

Tychon Moiseievych made a sarcastic comment on this point as well, and yet from this time on he began to observe me carefully and, occasionally, he would pose questions that apparently were intended to test the veracity of my claim.

Once, when Tychon and I were the only ones in the office, as he sat at the side table writing in his books, he suddenly began talking out loud, as if to himself. At first I didn't pay attention to what he was saying (or in what language), but when, after a few sentences, Tychon rose and started to walk about the room, gesticulating dramatically, I raised my head and began to pay attention. At first none of it made any sense but after a while I caught something familiar in Tychon's speech:

"From the farthest corners of the world, that is how it is … always news of affronts, conflicts, plunder, that is how it is …." Tychon recited in Ukrainian. And then he began to sing:

> "Each city has its own manners and its own laws
> Each head has its own mind
> Each person's desires lead him by the nose
> Each person's demons lure him on with lies"

Tychon Moiseievych would glance at me from time to time, checking to see how I would react. As I began to chuckle and, at the appropriate moment, responded with the appropriate line, perhaps not precise, but close in meaning, from the well-known Ukrainian operetta, "Natalka Poltavka," Tychon Moisejevych dropped his role-playing, and smiling at me, he said, "Now I believe that you really are a Ukrainian." But our conversation was cut short by someone who walked into the office.

Tychon Moiseievych's outward behavior toward me remained unchanged. He continued to play the clown, entertaining the office personnel with his stupid jokes. Just as before, he made caustic remarks about the "aristocratic" habits of the political deportees. Just as before, he tried to frightened me with stories about wolves, precisely at the time I was about to leave for my solitary walk home through the steppe. On the other hand, I noticed that when he measured out for me the ration of wheat that was so essential for our continued life's existence, he would add an extra measure. And he now filled the kerosene can to the rim, not halfway as he had before. Once, he even informed me that someone had brought in some frozen fish to sell and that I could buy some, even though until then such opportunities were open only to the local population, not the deportees. He did these things, but without altering his somewhat coarse outward behavior towards me.

Occasionally, when he was sure that no one else was in the office or nearby, he questioned me about the Ukrainians from Western Ukraine, although I sensed that he didn't believe everything I told him. Once when someone sent me a copy of "The Kobzar,"[10] from home I offered to lend him the book. He gladly accepted my offer, although he was very careful to make certain that no one had noticed our quiet arrangement.

The brutal, hungry and cold winter finally passed. Summer arrived. The war with Germany introduced a new element to the mood of the settlement (and therefore to our office as well). Naturally, as in the past, no one ventured opinions on the topic, nor did anyone ask unnecessary questions, yet there was an aura of some expected change. Then the mobilization of troops began.

As I came into the office one time, I noticed first an unfamiliar liveliness and disarray among the personnel. Then an overpowering, strong scent of cologne and perfume struck me. The smell was so overwhelming that it made my head spin. I first thought that the senior accountant had simply used too much cologne, but it quickly became apparent that the reason lay elsewhere. I noticed, first, that outside the office window a bunch of children was playing with an entire battery of empty cologne bottles. Then the elated mood of my co-workers, and their reddened faces explained the rest. In connection with the military mobilization a ban on the sale of alcohol had been declared, but the

---

10 "The Kobzar": the complete published collection of poems by Taras Shevchenko, the national bard-poet of Ukraine.

ingenious enthusiasts of hard liquor found their own solutions: sipping the not too palatable but very fragrant colognes.

Before long, Tychon Moiseievych, also in an elated mood, came into the office, radiating a full bouquet of multifaceted scents. Cracking jokes and clowning, he whirled about the office.

It appeared that he had been drafted. At one point he came up to me and, stammering a bit, he began what sounded like a farewell speech. Grasping my shoulder he forced me into a chair with him.

"So," he said, "Uliana Vladimirivna, I go to fight for our Soviet fatherland. I ask you, please, be good to my children. Do not let them forget who they are. And do not think badly of me; I just have this sharp tongue."

He continued to babble on in a confused fashion for a long time, and then, in parting, he added, "If you ever come across some especially caustic soap, you'll know that it was made from my bones—it's just because I have all this venom in me."

So much for Tychon Moiseievych. The next day after all the colognes had evaporated from people's heads, so that even the faintest scent had disappeared, he appeared in the office, the same as always. Cracking his usual and offensive jokes about the upper class, and how he's off to kill them, he said his goodbyes to us. Not too long afterwards, I moved to another settlement and so I had no way of reminding his children of who they were. Later I learned that Tychon Moiseievych had died in the war.

Chapter Ten:
Pasha Kopieikina

Pasha was the office cleaning lady. She had a "me-and-the-boss" kind of attitude because the director of the roads district, Jan Damazovich, frequently patted her on her back. She would come into the office and, propping her elbows up on the nearest desk, she would gab with all the employees of the division—the accountant, the engineer and even Jan Damazovich, whether the others had work to do or not. Whenever she had anything to say or brag about—for example, how she unglued the material from the back of a map of the Soviet Union and used it to make a dress for her daughter—everyone had to listen to Pasha.

"This is Soviet democracy," I thought, "Jan Damazovich the director and Pasha Kopieikina, the cleaning lady, conversing like equals."

Pasha looked down on me from a most exalted height. Actually, it was not so much that Pasha looked down on me as that she looked directly through me. To her I was not a some*one*, but rather a some*thing*. From her perspective I was on the very lowest rung of the social ladder, and she—well, she was up at the top, very close to Jan Damazovich.

But then winter arrived with its freezing cold and its accompanying shortages of food and it erected a barrier between Jan Damazovich and Pasha that no amount of back patting could erase. Jan Damazovich, the director and party member had access to special food supplies. Pasha, on the other hand didn't have enough food to feed her children. And then the social ladder took on a different complexion. Then Pasha's place on it fell closer to mine and farther from Jan Damazovich. But she hadn't grasped that at first.

Snow fell and our village was cut off from the rest of the world. In vain the district plows struggled, trying to keep the roads clear. If the roads were clear, the supplies came through. As new snow fell, more snow drifts would cut us off again. Again, the plows labored to clear the roads. Again, we hoped for the transports to make it through. So it went for months.

As winter progressed, Pasha's skin grew more sallow and she grew thinner. She became less animated. Sometimes she would deign to speak to me. Her social boundaries were shifting.

Then early spring arrived. The ice on the river had softened and then it cracked. The bridge became unsafe. Those travelers who needed to get to the other side decided to camp out on the river bank instead. Locals ventured out to investigate the campers, motivated not only by curiosity, but also in hopes that they might have some food supplies to trade—maybe even flour.

Pasha was among them. She would report back to the office what she had seen there: the condition of the bridge, the travelers, who they were, what goods could be obtained. But this was not the same talkative, self-confident Pasha as before. Her round face with its perky little nose had become elongated and her nose grew more pronounced.

One time she returned from the river unusually animated and energized. Her eyes sparkled. She talked on and on about some elderly, apparently well-to-do couple that she met there. Why did she find them so interesting? At first she didn't want to talk about that. Then finally, unable to restrain herself, she told us: they had wheat, bags and bags of wheat—and even flour! This was just sensational! Weren't they afraid that someone might rob them of it? But why should other people's wheat concern Pasha?

As Pasha began to explain, her voice grew distant. It was not clear if she was explaining the situation to those who worked in the office, or asking their advice, or simply stating facts.

"They want to take one of my daughters in exchange for the wheat and flour. That way I will be able to feed my other children. There will be enough to last us until summer."

A stunned silence filled the office. A moment passed before Jan Damazovich spoke thickly, "What are you saying Pasha? Do you mean to sell your child?"

Pasha flinched. Then almost immediately, her words came flying like gun shots, reminding us of the scrappy Pasha of the previous fall.

"Well, what am I supposed to do? Is it better if they all starve to death? She will be fine there. They're lonely, childless and prosperous."

Pasha was speaking quickly and loudly. Maybe she was trying to convince herself. Maybe she thought the louder the argument, the more sense it would make.

Jan Damazovich looked like he still wanted to say something. His lips moved but issued no sounds. Then thinking better of it, he just shrugged and left the office. He looked like he was washing his hands of this affair. Pasha stopped talking for a while, as if struck dumb. Everyone in the office was quiet. It seemed that no one knew what to say—or even what to think.

The travelers continued to camp out by the river for a few more days. Perhaps Pasha was getting flour or other supplies from them; she became lively, stopping at the office for short periods and then disappearing. She didn't chat much now. She was probably hurrying off to the riverbank, or maybe she went home to her children.

Occasionally she would attempt to explain and justify herself. Now the office workers were no longer silent as they had been when they first learned of her intention. Now they all spoke, expressing opinions, and offering advice as to whether it was right for Pasha to trade her child for a bag of flour or not. Some were for the exchange and others were against. But in the end, no amount of talk would feed Pasha's children.

The road was finally cleared. The travelers moved on. Things seemed to return to normal. But Pasha was no longer the same vivacious and talkative woman. Jan Damazovich's back pats no longer provided her with the same obvious satisfaction. Sometimes she would even talk to me. It seems that her ideas about the social ladder had undergone a transformation down by the river where those who camped there took her little daughter in exchange for one or maybe two bags of flour.

Chapter 11:

An Enchanted Night

Each of our work days lasted long into the night. When we were finally permitted to leave, I always found myself dreading the long walk home. For a kilometer and a half I had to make my way among the ruined and abandoned houses that bordered on the open steppe. These *rozvaliushky,* as we called them, were all that remained of the government's campaign against the *kulaks*—the wealthy peasants. After the authorities forcibly removed them, their houses, which had been constructed of unfired bricks, gradually fell apart in the rain and the snow. Here and there, a house still stood among the ruins, but all were dark now. Since we lived at the very edge of the village, bordering on the steppe, there were no other inhabited houses on my long walk home.

All my co-workers were Siberians; they were local people and they lived in the roads division housing next to the office building. They knew well that I dreaded my solitary walk home and yet, in conversation amongst themselves, they would "casually" bring up stories of wolves coming very close to houses during the harsh winters.

One day, trying to disregard their scary talk, I buttoned my old Lviv coat tightly, wrapped a scarf around my head, and headed for the door. As soon as I opened it, a steamy cloud of warm air burst out into the cold night. I hesitated at the door for a few seconds, but feeling the mocking gaze of my "comrade-workers" on my back, I drew the coat even more tightly around me and stepped out into the dark. This coat which I hadn't allowed to be sewn with a double liner (because I wanted to look slim) provided only poor protection against the cold. This night's temperature no doubt had fallen down to 40 degrees below. The only parts of my body that were warm were my feet, clad as they were in *valianky*—heavy felt boots—which we managed to exchange for some "European-style" clothing.

Outside, the office windows lights shone like yellow splotches. I passed them quickly and then headed out onto the main road. High above, the moon shone brightly. Crystalline shards of snow, illuminated by the moonshine, made the road glisten. The frozen snow squeaked quietly beneath my feet along the well-tamped path near the government building. I hurried past the roads district and quickly came upon the *rozvaliushky*.

The snowfall had been heavy that winter so the ruined and snow-covered structures and the dark shadows of their grotesque shapes contrasted sharply against the bright moonlight. Dark holes that once were doors held mysterious secrets. The more I stared at the shadows the more they seemed to come alive. Their shapes and their intense darkness seemed to shift subtly. Despite myself, I remembered the wolf stories and I began to see slinking, wolf-like silhouettes amid the darkened ruins.

Transfixed by the ruins and looking around to my right and left, I picked up my pace as much as possible. My footsteps squeaked louder. I turned onto the still untrod snowy path.

Suddenly, I heard the squeak of snowy footsteps behind me—coming faster and faster—as if someone were following me.

Danger needs to be looked directly in the eye. I stopped and looked around. But there was no one there. The snow-covered road continued to glisten. Silence, nothing, no sound of footsteps, not mine, not that of others. I went on—once more there was a squeak of snow—beneath my feet and behind me. Once more, standing in place, I looked around. The shadows that lived amid the ruined houses lay on the ground, silence surrounded me. Only the moon, high above me cold and indifferent, seemed to be watching me with a malevolent smile. At last, when I started walking once more and heard the squeak of snow again, I finally understood. It was the super-cooled air that carried an echo of my footsteps. I went on, a little calmer, but still afraid of the shadows lurking between the *rozvaliushky*.

Far ahead of me something ran across the road. Was it a wolf or a dog? I stopped and waited until it disappeared. Fear pierced me. Yet I still had to go on. The closer I came to where I had seen the creature, the more terrified I felt; my feet slowed of their own volition. I reached the spot; nothing here but whiteness and quiet all around. I passed it and again I quickened my pace. I was halfway home; soon I would see the house where Mother was waiting for me. No doubt she hadn't lit the lamp, because we had to conserve the kerosene, but she was waiting and accompanying me in her thoughts from *rozvaliushka* to *rozvaliushka*.

Suddenly, a vigorous new sound rang out, cutting through the silvery silence of the night that until then had been interrupted only by the squeaks of my *valianky*. Someone was singing! A hearty male baritone voice reverberated from somewhere beyond the *rozvaliushky*. The Ukrainian Classic, "Reve Ta Stohne Dnipr Shyrokyj" echoed across the entire breadth of the frozen sky.

I stopped, bewitched. Suddenly everything around me was transformed, as if touched by a magic wand. No longer was the moon cold, distant and evil. It became the friendly, romantic silvery face that, scattering crystal diamonds all around, was lighting my path home. The *rozvaliushky* became fantastic castles and their shadows no longer held awful secrets.

The voice slowly drifted away, and even though it grew softer and softer, I could hear it all the way home. By then the frigid air bore from afar another song to me:

> *"Oh moon, dear moon, do not shine for anyone else,*
> *shine only for my beloved when he goes walking home."*

Chapter: 12

Toujours l'Amour

It *is* possible to talk about love endlessly. Women in particular can and do discuss it throughout their lives, regardless of age. First they dream about love, then they experience it—maybe even suffer because of it—and finally, they look back and reminisce.

It would seem that only dreamers, the kind of people whose lives are filled with poetry and music, are capable of experiencing deep and genuine love, full of sacrifice and self-denial. For them the real world represents an unendurable burden with which they cannot cope. But in fact, it is frequently quite the opposite. It often seems that it's these very dreamers, who while questing for the "ideal," more often than not, repeatedly change the object of their affection and experience more than one "eternal" love—while it's the realists who, having fallen in love once, commit the rest of their lives to its deep feelings.

It's about this latter kind of love that I want to tell you.

On normal weekdays the Sokil-Batko Field in Lviv was the site of sports training, games, and physical exercise. On holidays and special occasions it was the venue for field and track competitions, soccer and volleyball games, scholastic gymnastic events and Plast celebrations. Regardless, whether a normal weekday or a special event, it was always a place where young people, interested in sports or not, would gather. Some would exercise and compete while others would simply look on as spectators. It was always a place free of worry, full of enthusiasm, filled with fun and games. What an appropriate place for young people to meet!

There was some sort of celebration taking place on the field. A well-disciplined school marching band, arranged in neat rows, was going through its routines. Sometimes the crowd would pay attention to what was happening on the field and sometimes people just strolled along the dusty paths that ran along the wall that surrounded the field. There were crowds of children around the cold drink and ice cream stands. Young people, groups of girls and boys, tossed jests back and forth among themselves. Like balls, the volleys of banter flew from one side to the other, and then back again culminating in shouts and explosions of laughter.

Amid this relaxed assemblage, two pairs of eyes—the blue eyes of a cheerful, trim and fair-haired young man and the grey, heavily lashed eyes of a petite, dark-haired and black-browed girl—met, unaware that this moment would be the beginning of a turbulent love story. A small yellowish spot on one of the girl's irises seemed to enlarge her pupils and gave her eyes an unusual, focused appearance. She seemed to observe everything very closely and therefore appeared capable of seeing more than others. His quick movements, his hearty laughter and his impassioned speech betrayed an athletic personality.

This was their first meeting, but there would be others—all at the same Sokil-Batko field. Eventually the meetings led to escorted walks home, first with a group and then as a couple. Soon they understood that this was love. It would seem then that the story should have ended here—beginning as it did so simply and as do so many others. But it was not to be.

First, for some reason their parents objected. It seems that since the dawn of time parents have always found their children's choices inappropriate. Sometimes the reasons might have to do with some aspect of family background, or the social environment or maybe wealth. Or simply that for one's own dear child, *any* prospective fiancé always seems somehow "imperfect."

It isn't exactly clear why their parents (Yurko's? or maybe Hanusia's?) objected. What is important is that their love did not yield to the objection. They simply decided to postpone getting married until they were financially independent.

But the war managed to do that which their parents could not—it separated the young lovers. Yurko's father was arrested and then he and his mother were deported to Kazakhstan.

*****

The villages in Kazakhstan are spaced many kilometers apart. Nevertheless, somehow, by some means, news managed to travel from one deportee settlement to another. Sometimes the reports had to make their way via Lviv, but even when all connections with our native city were severed, still somehow the exchange of news continued. And so we learned (via Lviv) that a mother and her son Yurko, our acquaintances from home, were living in one of the villages in our district. On the heels of that letter, we got another bit of information, one that seemed to be lifted from one of those old Tsarist-era stories that I heard from my grandmother, where women voluntarily chose to join husbands and sweethearts who had been exiled to Siberia in order to share in their trials and hardships. It sounded so romantic to me, like a fairy tale. Hanusia had chosen to leave Lviv in order to follow Yurko to Kazakhstan.

I didn't know Hanusia but I very much wanted to meet this romantic figure. One day, our *kolhosp* was sending a supply convoy to the railroad station. The village in which Yurko's family lived was along the way—so I gladly volunteered for the assignment.

I vividly remember the house at Worker's Row, as well as the first time I saw Hanusia. I had imagined that I would find some dreamy nymph. I was greeted by a petite yet energetic young woman who greeted me warmly with a firm handshake. The bold expression of her eyes that looked directly into mine instilled confidence and trust.

Their home displayed clear evidence of her arrival. And it was not only a matter of the household articles that she was able to bring with her—things that no one could bring during a hurried and forced evacuation. There was an atmosphere of optimism here. One might even say that this was a "normal" home—albeit situated in a different geographical locale and under more primitive circumstances. There was none of the despair, resignation, and abnegation that oppressed, threatened and broke so many others here. Having to struggle constantly with these was for each of us, unbearably difficult.

The very fact that it was possible to cross those thousands and thousands of kilometers—and that they were traveled by a young woman—made the distance seem shorter somehow. Moreover, here was a person who not long ago had walked the streets of Lviv, breathed its air and maybe even physically saw with her own eyes those special people who, for us, were now merely the objects of our dreams. There was no end to my questions, but our time together was short. I had to return to the transport.

If Hanusia and Yurko had fallen in love at first sight, so also our friendship began at first sight. In spite of—or maybe because of—the fact that our personalities were somehow different, our friendship managed to survive the Siberian blizzards and the oppressive summer heat; it survived all the tragedies and all the misfortunes that we had to endure.

At first we exchanged letters. And then taking advantage of a brief period of eased conditions for political deportees, we moved to the same settlement where Yurko and his family lived. Through our shared daily experiences, our friendship deepened.

At the edge of the village there was a *kolhosp* where the so-called *spetsy* lived. The term "*spetsy*" applied to political deportees of the de-kulakization period. These *spetsy* came from the Leningrad area. They lived in long, grey, barracks which had an outward appearance of impoverished hovels. But the *spetsy* had formed a well-structured community. Not only were they amazingly capable of dealing with the challenges of the natural environment, but even more, they were able to organize their work so that both "the wolf was sated, and the goat was whole."[11] They knew how to manage their government quota requirements so something was always left over for them. On the surface they appeared to be poorer-than-poor, but all our belongings—our clothing, our linens etc—had a way of disappearing into their chests in exchange for food supplies.

Hanusia and I would go there some evenings to exchange our dresses or other belongings for milk. Along the way we had long heart-to-heart talks; it was then that I heard about her meeting Yurko at the

---

11   Ukrainian proverb similar in meaning to "having your cake and eating it too."

Batko-Sokil Field and the complete history of their love all the way up to her arrival here in Siberia. Most memorable was her simple response to my question about her decision to come here.

"We loved each other—and so this was, logically, just the next step, simply its natural consequence."

My God! Just a natural consequence—for a young girl to leave behind everything that was near and dear to her? To come here, into this terrible wilderness, to face an unknown present and an uncertain future?

To come to this place was more than a mere decision or a simple commitment. It wasn't simply a matter of "getting on a train and going." Hanusia had to overcome many obstacles. There were so many difficulties in obtaining an official government permission to relocate. All the painstaking attempts—even the subterfuge—all the hopes and disappointments! And still, she came here very well prepared. Letters from Kazakhstan had let her know what to expect and she brought with her everything that might be needed, beginning with the clothing—the *valyanky*, the padded trousers, the ear-flap-caps, the lamb's wool coats for Yurko, his mother and herself. She even brought a windowpane! They had written that the glass in the window of their hut was broken and that it was impossible to find glass to replace it—so she brought the pane.

But that wasn't all. Hanusia did not neglect anything. Foremost among her belongings was a solemn matrimonial certificate documenting her marriage to her separated-by-thousands-of-kilometers betrothed. And the certificate even contained a special blessing by Metropolitan Sheptytsky! She did not forget anything. Nothing that she did was casual, improvised, or unforeseen. Every step was a logical, practical, and intentional consequence of her great love.

The long journey by train was marked by many transfers and stops along the way. None of it was without incident. Finally she reached the station that was to be the end of her rail travel. She was expecting to find Yurko waiting for her there but her message of arrival had been delayed. She and Yurko missed each other. As it happened, a freight truck was going to the village where Yurko lived with his mother, and the driver agreed to take her. The name of the village was *Ush-Ahash* ("Three Trees"), although in fact there was not a single shrub around.

When the truck finally arrived at the village, the driver unloaded the freight and told her to get off. She thought she had been let out in the middle of a pure wilderness. The squat, gray, flat roofed houses built of unbaked clay were barely visible, disappearing against the background of the steppe. The truck rode off and she began to look around, trying to distinguish one house from another. In one of them the window was covered with pasteboard. This had to be it! Yurko had written that their window pane was missing.

Indeed, inside she found Yurko's mother, who was just then playing solitaire and looking to the cards to predict whether or not Hanusia would actually arrive.

Although Yurko, being young and capable, would have managed reasonably well without her, nevertheless Hanusia, with her energy and her practicality—and given the fact that she was a politically "free" person and thus able to move about without restrictions—significantly lightened the family's situation. She took their fate into her own small and dynamic hands. More than anything else, what she brought was what so many of the political deportees, dragged down by a sense of despair and impermanence, lacked—a positive, pro-active attitude towards life. Her consistency, her tenacity and her courage were helpful not only for her own family but they re-instilled a sense of optimism in us all.

For me and my dear ones she arrived just at the time when illness, hunger and death were making their way into our house. Against these, we had no means of protecting ourselves. There was no relief from them, never mind victory over them.

Hanusia would frequently stop by at our house. The mere appearance of her small, boyish figure, dressed in her padded trousers, her sheepskin jacket and her ear-flap-cap, standing there in the doorway, was a consolation— it was the difference between empty-handed pity and a compassion full of willingness to help.

She would force me to leave my place there by the stove where I was constantly and vainly attempting to blow life into the smoldering dung-patty, trying to force an actual flame from it. I don't know whether it was the fault of our stove, or the wet fuel or just because maybe I didn't know how to make the *kyziak* burn; whatever the reason, our living space was always filled with an acrid smoke that made breathing difficult and caused my poor sick mother to cough incessantly.

Hanusia would drag me out into the frigid but fresh air, leading me from one place to another where she had heard that food was available. Her calm and her firmness, devoid of pointless words of sympathy, was like a life-saving branch for which a drowning person might grasp. I think that many times she would drag me out of the house—in a kind of tacit conspiracy with my family—as much to fill me with strength and a glimmer of hope for a brighter future as to search for the availability of food.

All of Hanusia's family sought to support us, but for me she was a special kind of talisman which, even if incapable of bringing outright happiness, was a source of protection against the worst of misfortunes. And for me the worst did come just when Hanusia was away. She had gone to fetch her father-in-law who had been released from prison camp.

Maybe that's how it had to be. I think, however, that she, armed in her love, was intended to be a talisman for her own family. Because while almost all deportee families, even those who were able to return to their own homelands (or to some other places in the civilized world) came back decimated, having left behind some of their dearest ones buried in the Siberian ground –sometimes in marked graves, sometimes not—this family, who were deported as two persons, came back as five. Not only was Yurko's father restored to them from his prison camp but a year later—or maybe two (I don't remember), Hanusia and Yurko had a baby boy.

He grew up—as did all my god-children—to be a fine young man.

Chapter 13:

God's Christmas Tree

(Dedicated to Oliusia Terletska-Smal)

Christmas, our first in these steppes of Kazakhstan, was approaching. Winter was raging. It was, perhaps, the fiercest of all the winters that we spent there. But maybe it only seemed that way to me; it was our first in this land and we were unaccustomed to its deep freezes and its snows.

The snow was so heavy that, for months in some places, you could touch the tops of telegraph poles by standing on top of a snow-drift. Sometimes a house would be so covered with snow that a tunnel needed to be dug to the entrance. Our neighbors, in order to enter or leave their house, had to open up a part of the roof to their adjoining stable and then use a ladder to climb down from the roof.

The roads too, were covered with drifts. Trucks had a very hard time making their way through, and then only in the wake of a snowplow. After a while, even that became impossible. Finally, it fell to the sturdy and patient oxen, pulling convoys of sleds, to deliver the mail that had arrived at the distant railroad station. Even so, the trip took between a week to ten days so that the eagerly awaited letters from Lviv arrived very rarely and very intermittently.

Packages had stopped coming altogether; they were probably being stored in warehouses along the way, awaiting more auspicious weather and cleared roads. These parcels had been enormously helpful for us. Now we had to make do with whatever we still had on hand—whatever we had managed to save from the preceding fall. Whoever did not have access to such provisions went hungry. Some people didn't survive the winter.

In the midst of this struggle for life, for food, for warmth another struggle was also being waged—against hopelessness and despair. Consequently it became unthinkable for us not to celebrate Christmas, to ignore the birth of the Son of God.

So how were we to prepare *Sviat-Vechir,* the solemn Holy Christmas Eve Supper? Well, perhaps not with the traditional twelve meatless dishes, but not in total hunger either. There were beets for the *borscht* and there was wheat for the ritual *kutia* (albeit without the honey). Someone had managed to get some frozen fish and kept it in our unheated room (a natural refrigerator) to preserve it for the holiday meal. Someone else had saved a few crystals of saccharine to sweeten the meal for a better future.

But what about a Christmas tree? In the barren steppe where we lived it was rare enough to find a poplar or a willow—and even these had been planted and cultivated by human hands. In our village there was only one solitary tree and it grew beside the only freshwater well. So how could we even begin to think about a fir tree? Nevertheless, there were those who refused to give up. Would you believe that a desiccated wormwood shrub—growing naturally tall and sturdy in these parts— might be preserved and serve as a sadly deformed Christmas tree? Human ingenuity and imagination knew no bounds. Long before Christmas, during every spare moment, we began making Christmas tree ornaments using packing materials from parcels that had been sent to us, from newspapers and from old textbooks. Objectively speaking these ornaments probably were not very pretty— yet consider how much imagination, deeply felt longing and love went into their making!

We received a miniature Christmas tree constructed from two hard book covers; it had been given to us by two elderly women who were no longer capable of hard manual labor. Their patient hands had drawn boughs, cut them out, and cleverly glued them together to create a three-dimensional tree. Then they painted it green using paint salvaged from an old parcel. Painted dried peas, made to look like Christmas balls, were suspended by bits of thread. Attached to the tips of the "boughs" were tiny little twigs that represented candles. The only things that the tree lacked were size and the characteristic scent of fir.

More than anything else, we needed news from home—from our dear family and friends. Every day I would hurry home from work, plowing my way through the deep snow, with only one thought on my mind: would there be any mail? If so, Mother would put the letter (or the package, if there was one) in a visible location so that it could delight me as soon as I entered the room. If there was a parcel, mother would first satisfy her own curiosity by untying the strings and removing the top wrapping material, but then she would put everything back exactly as the senders' hands had packed it. She wanted us to experience the same joy in unpacking it as she had.

Of course, since the heavy winter snowfalls all such delights came to a halt. Instead, my own experience of daily hope and disappointment was not unlike that of the Ukrainian poet Shevchenko who, during his exile, wrote, "And again, I have no mail from Ukraine."

On January 1, New Years Day, it began to snow once more—a windless snowstorm. Huge quiet flakes thickly blanketed the layers of snow previously tamped down. It made walking to work even harder as I had to make a new path in the new snow that reached over my knees. The next day the snow finally stopped. The moon was almost full and I, having to work late, could make my way home by the light of the moon that night. Everything glistened in the silvery crystalline moonlit snow.

On Christmas Eve[12] I managed to leave work a little earlier, happy that I could make it home before it was too late. The moon had not risen yet. The sky had taken on a dark blue, almost purple hue, but where the sun had just set, a bright golden streak lit up the horizon. By the time I neared home, the first evening star had appeared.[13] In spite of myself, I stopped, and gazing at it, thought of all those people back home who also were looking for the first star—although, perhaps, in a different

---

12   Christmas Eve falls on January 6 according to the Julian calendar.

13   By tradition the Christmas Eve meal cannot begin until the first evening star makes its appearance in the sky. Usually it is the children who search the sky, impatient for the star to appear.

constellation. The star was wondrously bright and it twinkled in the frosty sky. It seemed to me that with each step that I took, it moved with me; it was leading me home. A sense of the grandeur and infinity of the heavens fused with a sudden awareness of the distance that separated us from our real home. Overwhelmed by yearning and sorrow, I knocked on the door, and shaking off the snow from my *valyanky* I entered with the traditional Christmas greeting: "*Khrystos Rozhdayetsia*!"—"Christ is Born!"

Immediately I was struck by unusual warmth. Obviously, tonight we were heating our home with more than our usual ration of fuel. The room seemed festively ornate. The tiny cardboard Christmas tree cast a realistically long shadow on the rime-covered walls. And it wasn't just this shadow that touched me—there was a scent of fir in the air. It was then that I saw the letters and the package. They were laid out on the festively spread white tablecloth. Without even removing my coat, and under the smiling gaze of my mother, I leapt for the package. There on the very top, wrapped in thin tissue paper was a piece of *Prosphora*[14] and, next to it, a sprig of fir. Oliusia, my dearest and truest friend in the whole world, had sent us this package. It was a heart-wrapped, not a hand-wrapped package, as my father once wrote from his prison camp.

Such wonderful things it contained! Every single item was skillfully wrapped and carefully marked to let us know whose gift it was. Even in this, Oliusia's personality shone through. She was the one who mailed the parcel but if something in the package was a gift from someone else as well, she made a note of it so that all the gratitude would not be directed to her alone. We knew how difficult it was to send such a parcel. Often it was necessary to travel quite a distance to a town where packages being sent to Kazakhstan were accepted for delivery. Among the contents, to be shared commonly by all, there was also special medication for Mother. Seeing the handwriting on the little box, I recognized it as Oliusia's. She was a pharmacist and she had prepared the medication herself.

And so, the distance between us that had so overwhelmed me earlier with its immensity somehow suddenly shrank. And although I have no

14 Prosphora= the previously blessed bread consumed at the beginning of the Christmas Eve supper.

rational explanation for it, I know that it had to be Oliusia's goodness that cleared the way for those sturdy and patient oxen so that they could deliver this package on this very night.

The sprig of fir that Oliusia's good hands had placed in the box, filled the room with an aroma of Christmas and of our native home. It brought to life the cardboard Christmas tree and it cast a shadow of God's own tree onto the cold walls of our house. And when we sang our ancient carol, *"Boh Predvichniy"*—"Eternal God"—our decidedly non-concert-caliber voices knocked down the walls of our house, broke out of the embrace of this tiny, God-forsaken Siberian village and flew thousands of kilometers westward. I saw our dear, dear family and friends standing around us—my father's slender figure and my Oliusia's voice caroling along with us.

Chapter 14:

Kariss

"*Kariss*" is the Kazakh word for silk, yet I never saw any of this silk during my time in Kazakhstan. Maybe somewhere in some isolated village, some elderly Kazakh woman had hidden away a remnant of this luxuriant Asian fabric and preserved it in her chest. However, when I was there it was hard enough to get a piece of simple cotton or homespun linen. I only heard from others about this cloth's beauty and softness, about its amazing texture and its vibrant color.

But "Kariss" is also a Kazakh woman's name. Almost all Kazakh names have specific meanings. For example, "Balakhanum" means "Little Lady" and "Kulbanu" means "fragrance of rose" (although in these northeastern provinces of Kazakhstan it was unlikely that anyone had ever even seen a rose). So—Kariss was also a name, and it was the name of the still-young Kazakh woman in whose house I came to live. She was often called "Katya"—in the same way that many traditional Kazakh names were being Russified and transformed, into all kinds of "Galyas," "Shuras" and "Nyuras." Nevertheless it was she herself who told me that her name was Kariss and explained its meaning to me. So I called her Kariss and I noticed that it pleased her when I did. After all, who among us wouldn't want such a silken name?

Kariss' husband was no ordinary Kazakh who tended sheep or worked at the *kolhosp*. He must have had some education because he

73

worked at the Regional Financial Office. By the time I came to live in Kariss' house he had already been drafted at the very start of the war with Germany and was off fighting somewhere in Europe. Meanwhile Kariss was left alone with her three small children.

Kariss was pretty. Certainly she seemed that way to me in comparison to so many of her countrywomen with their slanted eyes, their protruding cheekbones and their fat little noses. But even objectively speaking, without making any comparisons, she stood out with her delicate features harmonizing so well with the expressiveness of her dark eyes. I think I would have judged her beautiful in an exotic and mysterious way anywhere in the world. Her movements were graceful, fluid and quick—yet always somehow controlled. Her hands and her feet were small like that of most Kazakh women. Her smile was a restrained smile, a half smile that strangely illuminated her face and kindled golden sparks in her eyes. But back then, Kariss smiled only rarely and I saw her truly happy only a very few times.

Although Kariss' husband was an office clerk—and therefore a member of the "educated worker" class, I think that her own education was limited to knowing how to read and write. Yet the way in which she carried herself made her stand out from among her Kazakh neighbors. There was a sensitivity about her that kept her from entering our room without warning—unlike all other Kazakh women. They would appear in groups, especially soon after we had just arrived, squat on their heels, leisurely lean against the wall of our room and, for hours, follow all our movements with their eyes and make comments in Kazakh that were (of course) unintelligible to us. Something like this would have been inconceivable for Kariss. Even if she were curious about us and how we lived, her curiosity never exhibited itself in that obvious and rude way.

True, Kariss was not always as "silky" as her name. Sometimes we could hear her angry voice through the wall, scolding her three children. Arguments with her neighbor flared up more than once. Then, a stream of the sharp, guttural sounds typical of the Kazakh language would pour from her lips. But really, these incidents were rare exceptions.

Kariss had three children. The eldest, Saken, was almost seven when we moved in. He was a small boy with an unusually long and pointed head; he was very active and alert, but to be honest, he was annoying and therefore not a very pleasant boy. In keeping with Kazakh tradition, it would have fallen to him to be the head of the household in his father's absence. He should have helped with his younger siblings, his little brother Arsen and his sister Sara, whenever his mother had to be away from home—which was often. Of course, he was no different than any other boy his age and he was always looking for an opportunity to get out of the house. His "baby sitting" most frequently ended with the younger children in tears. If we were at home, it fell to us to calm them and bring peace to these little Kazakhs.

The two younger children's appearance reflected the effects of poverty, which had become even more acute now that their father was away. Like so many Kazakhs—even adults—the middle child, four-year-old Arsen, was bowlegged, but he did have use of his legs. He had a swinging gait but it did not prevent him from walking or even running. The youngest, Sara, maybe two years old or so, was an extraordinarily thin little girl with pathetic little arms and malformed teeth—a result of rickets. Her skinny little legs were not even capable of supporting her body. She could crawl a little but she could not stand. The most poignant features of this little person were her beautiful brown eyes and the black locks of hair that surrounded her pale little face.

Kariss' house was a typical Kazakh dwelling. Some of the older houses in remote villages or even in the older parts of this village had more corridors and passageways, probably as a protection against the cold winds. However this house, like the others, was built of *saman*, sun-baked bricks, and covered by a flat clay-coated roof. The outer door, which was just a couple of pieces of wood hammered together, led to a larger entranceway that also served as a stable. It was occupied by two cows, whose milk was the main food source for Kariss and her children. Passing through the stable there was an inner door, slightly less rickety than the outer door, leading to Kariss' room and another one that connected to a tiny hallway that led to our room. The walls, though thick, provided little protection against the wind and the bitter cold because the unfired bricks absorbed moisture. The tiny windows were cemented into the walls, which prevented them from letting in fresh air in the summer and provided little protection against the cold of winter. Frost frequently coated the walls and thick ice patterns covered the windows. In the winter, we would cover the earthen floor with straw to make it warmer and during the summer months, we would daub it with clay from time to time, to keep it from crumbling.

The house was located on Steppe Street. Mostly Kazakhs inhabited this part of the village. Actually it would be hard to describe it as a "street," because the houses were strewn about in no particular order. The houses were laid out in this district as if someone had taken a fistful of seeds, opened his hand and let the seeds simply spill.

Of course, there were no fences, no shrubs, not even a single blade of grass. Here and there a wind-sown wormwood bush grew—and then dried up in the harsh summer's sun. All winter, in front of each house, there was a huge pile of cow manure that would be shoveled out of the stable. In the spring, the pile would "sweat" and steam until it was time to transform it into fuel. In the summer, each house had an outdoor clay fireplace with a cauldron built into it. These were the summer kitchens because it was too hot to cook indoors.

It would seem that ownership of two cows would have provided sufficient insurance against starvation. Yet it was not quite so simple, because the cows needed to be fed. Kazakh cows are small, and although their milk is rich, there isn't much of it—and they need to eat.

I think maybe Kariss took us in hoping that we would help her in providing feed for the cows. My brother was working at the *kolhosp* at the time and in payment he was eligible to receive straw, if not hay. Piling up straw against the walls protected us against the cold and we could burn it for fuel. We would spread out the straw over the clay floor every day, and then, in the evening, we would gather and burn it to cook our meals and heat the room, laying out fresh straw for the following day. It became apparent that whenever we were out of the house Kariss' cows would be helped to an extra portion of feed—our straw! But what could we do?

After my brother was drafted into the "labor army" I was left alone. There was no more straw and no man around the house to help Kariss with her work. I spent an additional winter with her. We were two solitary women, separated not only by a physical wall but also by so many psychological differences, coming as we did from two different worlds and representing different races and cultures. Still, we were bound by a similar anxiety for our absent loved ones. She was filled with worry for her husband, fighting a war somewhere in distant Europe, and

I for my father and brothers away somewhere in labor camps or in far off, unknown places. We were two women who had to struggle for all of life's essentials, for every piece of bread, for basic physical survival—and we were sustained by our memories and our hopes for a better future.

Often during the winter months in the evening, as I sat reading or mending my clothes by the light of a lamp that I had improvised from a bottle, there in the night's silence I would hear Kariss singing quietly. Do you know the musical composition, "In a Persian Market"? Its main theme has to be the Kazakh melody that I could hear Kariss humming on the other side of the wall. The words to Kazakh songs are rather simple and sparse. Frequently they are improvised on the spot, describing what is happening at the time. For example they might be, "there's a camel coming" or "the child sleeps," and then the phrase would be repeated again and again. I could never make out the words to Kariss' song but the melody was one filled with longing and sadness and as monotonously haunting as the steppe around us.

Occasionally Kariss would come over to talk. She would talk about old Kazakh customs or about her husband. Her parents and her family had all been nomads. In the summer, they lived in yurts, moving around, following the seasons and availability of pastures. They lived in permanent homes only during the winter. The women were subservient to men and veiled their faces. We could see the remnants of those dress traditions among some older Kazakh women—the white scarves that they wound around their heads. In addition, it was understood, that a wife, in serving the men in the family had to wait until they had had their fill before she and the children could eat the leftovers. This they had to consume separately, never in the presence of the men, and above all—God forbid—never, ever in the presence of guests. These examples of the subjugation of Kazakh women, both great and small, are typical of the not too distant past. If I mention them now, it's only because it struck me that although Kariss' mother was a mere shadow of her husband, yet she did not have to struggle for anything on her own or make any decisions on her own. She was not, nor was she allowed to be, an independent and fully responsible human being. Perhaps an old matriarch of a clan might be permitted to have some voice, but it was only as the guardian of traditions, the voice of the one who had raised and taught her sons how to organize their lives and her daughters to submit and obey.

Now, one generation later, Kariss found herself alone with her children in extremely difficult circumstances. It is true that sometimes a male family member would come and help her with some of the physical tasks like spreading out the manure and transforming it into fuel. Once someone helped her re-coat the roof of her house with clay. Later, after she had not heard from her husband for a long time, a representative of her clan appeared and tried to persuade Kariss to marry a male member of her husband's family. This would have been in accordance with Kazakh custom which demanded that a deceased man's brother marry the dead man's widow. Kariss refused. She firmly believed that her husband, of whom she spoke with love and admiration, would return. She would try to ensure the necessary sustenance for herself and her children on her own. Therefore, she alone bore the full burden of providing food for her family.

Day by day, she would go into the village, taking things with her to sell in exchange for food. In time, we joined forces in these "commercial" ventures for necessities. True, our circumstances were different. I had to work, while Kariss, being the wife of a man serving in the military, received a small pension and ration cards for bread. But neither source was sufficient to live on. It was impossible to buy flour or other staple foods with my salary alone and Kariss' bread subsidy cards, frequently remained just that—cards. More than once whenever one of us would learn about some place where it might be possible to exchange goods for food, we would share that information with each other.

In the spring, Kariss would go out to the fields to glean whatever wheat was leftover from the previous harvest. It was forbidden to glean immediately after the fall harvest; the penalty for doing so was the same as for theft. However in spring, the administration tended to look the other way at such activities; so Kariss would go. She would bring home the grain ears in a sack, thrash the sack with a cudgel and then winnow away the chaff by some primitively devised means. She then would roast the wheat kernels, grind them down in a mortar and put them through a sifter. The finer ground meal would be soaked in milk to become a staple of Kazakh food called *tolkan*, while the more course kernels were referred to as *kurmash*.

Whenever Kariss would leave her children alone she would leave them with a handful of *kurmash* and a lump of butter. The *kurmash* was roasted and crunchy so it was too hard for little Sara's rickety teeth. More than once, when I was at home, I would hear Sara crying in the other room and go to investigate. I would find Sara crying, unable to chew the *kurmash* because of her sore gums.

On occasion, if I happened to have some bread I would share little pieces of it with the children. These were not whole slices—unfortunately, there wasn't enough bread for that. These were just little pieces about half the size of a finger. When dividing the bread I had to be extra careful to be sure that all portions were exactly the same size. Arsen kept a very careful watch and he would protest loudly if anything seemed unfairly divided. If only one child was at home and got a piece of bread or a carrot or something of the sort, I could be sure that as soon as the others learned of it they would immediately appear in my room, waiting for their "allotment." Then, in the evening, when their mother came home, I could hear them telling her about what they had received. It was painful to hear these poor children talk about a tiny piece of bread as if it were something special.

From time immemorial the main staple of the Kazakh diet had been meat—usually lamb or well-marbled mutton. They also ate flour-based foods like flatbreads, the *tolkan* and the *kurmash*. They used milk to make butter and a hard cheese. With these foods, they drank tea, which they prepared especially well. All other foods they regarded as "grass." Now their favorite foods were no longer available.

I tried to persuade Kariss to cook the wheat into a porridge that could be eaten with milk or butter. She tried cooking it if she had the time. Whenever I had beets or cabbage, I would give her some to taste. Once I got hold of some meat and cabbage stew somewhat similar to the *bigos* we made at home and invited her to share it with me. After the very first spoonful, she stopped, motionless, and I saw that she did not know whether she should swallow it or spit it out. I finally guessed her dilemma. No matter how hungry she was, she was afraid that the stew contained pork. For Kazakhs pork is not only forbidden by their religion, but is, in itself, considered disgusting. I have to admit that I lied, telling her that it was some other meat—maybe camel. Then, she ate her portion but with some hesitancy.

As spring approached, we tried to convince Kariss to plant a vegetable garden near the house. Without too much enthusiasm, she planted some beets, carrots and something else. The problem was that the garden needed water, water drawn from the deep village well that gradually dried up as the summer advanced. Nevertheless, by the time summer arrived, Kariss' little vegetable beds sported some vibrant greenery and there were enough vegetables for soup. Together with a friend, I began to teach Kariss how to make *borshch*.

It was already hot so our lessons were being conducted outdoors in the summer kitchen. Other Kazakh women, from the neighboring houses, gathered to observe the cooking class. Children gathered round the outdoor stove, holding their bowls and spoons in their hands, little Sara the first among them—long before the *borshch* was ready. Kariss listened to our instructions carefully and seriously. The thick *borshch* was certainly delicious (and would have been even more so if it had been well-seasoned with sour cream), but I am not sure if the Kazakhs liked it very much, unaccustomed as they were to eating vegetables. For them, I think, it was just a "necessary evil," not a tasty meal in itself.

Even though Kariss had grown fond of me and my friend who joined me in the spring after my brother left, she asked us to find other housing. She had a prospective tenant who, as had my brother, worked at the *kolhosp*. Moreover he was a relative, and he could help her with getting feed for the cows. We found another room to live in and Kariss and I parted company—I must say—with mutual regret.

I still came to visit her, to see how she was doing, and especially to ask if she had any news of her husband. There was no news. Her family tried to convince her that there was no reason to wait any longer. No news had to mean that he was no longer alive. Kariss was young, and despite the difficulties and hard work that wore her down, she was advised to find herself another man—maybe even a relative—to marry her.

Embarrassed, Kariss spoke of this to me with lowered eyes; she didn't even want to consider the possibility of being unfaithful to her husband, who might still be alive somewhere. Hope was rekindled when the men of the village started coming home from the war. First the wounded returned, and then, following them, some that had been demobilized. They brought with them war "trophies"—various curiosities—from

Germany. Kariss quizzed them: had any of them seen her husband, had they heard anything about him? There was some news brought back by the returnees, but only in whispers and repeated only to those who could be trusted: soldiers who had been taken as prisoners of war by the Germans were not permitted to return home. They were put in prison camps as politically unreliable.

Each homecoming was unique because each person was unique—both the returnee and the one awaiting him. Each one had been affected by unique experiences and unique reactions to those experiences. Still, it can be said that there were some joyful reunions where both sides had faithfully looked forward to the return and listened with sympathy and understanding to each other's ordeals. Then there were the disappointing homecomings, where there was no one to welcome the veterans home. In some cases there were instances where the elapsed time had completely changed the individuals and their approach to life, love and the world. The Red Army had conquered parts of Europe. Its soldiers had, in one way or another, seen the lives of people who lived in those conquered territories. Although viewed in the light of flames and violence, some aspects of the old ways of life were still evident. Semi-literate villagers wrote letters home, expressing their impressions of the conquered lands. In one, a young Kazakh, writing from beautiful Krakow, lamented how much he missed the gray steppe of Kazakhstan. For him this lovely ancient city was not in the least bit beautiful, instead it seemed monstrous and alien. There were letters that simply described the houses, the kitchens, the apartments, the stores, women's clothing, without mentioning the boulevards, the churches, the parks. The writers of these letters said that when they returned they wanted to live differently. It sometimes happened that upon coming home a returning veteran would become deeply disillusioned. He no longer wanted a house that had to be entered by way of a stable. He was unhappy with the way his wife dressed and the simple food she prepared. He had become "infected" with Europe. Now he criticized everything that he once perceived as the ideal of beauty, domesticity and love. The men came home changed.

The women too, were no longer the same. Not only the ongoing struggle for food, but also the unrelenting difficulty in obtaining even the most minute necessities of life had to have changed them, both outwardly and inwardly. Besides, there had been rumors of robberies and rapes committed by the army in which their husbands served. Some women dreaded the return of their husbands.

Finally, the time arrived when I was allowed to leave Kazakhstan. I went to see Kariss again. My first question to her: was there any news about her husband?

"Yes, but it's very uncertain," she told me. "Someone had seen him; he was wounded. Perhaps he was taken prisoner by the Germans. So, there is still hope. Maybe he will return."

Kariss' eyes shone and a smile appeared on her lips, illuminating her face and erasing the marks of those difficult years. Finally, someone would discipline Saken; he was becoming more and more rebellious toward his mother. Finally, she would not have to struggle alone to get food for the family and feed for the cows. Then her smile faded and she asked simply, "But what will he be like when he returns? Will he leave me, like that one neighbor who left his wife, if he sees my beauty faded and worn? Will he be constantly angry and impatient, like the other neighbor who always talks about the wonders of distant lands and who now wants to move to the European part of the Soviet Union—but without his wife? Will he come back as a cripple?"

It was apparent from her comments that deep-seated feelings of inferiority and dependency were resurfacing. Kariss hadn't considered that although she was a nomad's daughter, totally unprepared for living on her own, she had already exhibited considerable strength of character and the ability to survive these difficult years. She hadn't considered how her husband had acted and how *he* had behaved; she only worried whether he would be willing to accept her as a wife in his home.

I tried to cheer her up as best I could. I reminded her how she always told me that he was different from others and that he loved her so much. What more could I do? We said our goodbyes and I departed.

What has happened to you now, Kariss? Did your Rakhman return? Has he taken away from you the heavy burden of that unremitting struggle for food? Or was he smitten with Europe? Does he remember other women and compare you to them?

I would advise you to smile at him in your half-sad way, to gaze at him from beneath the thick lashes of your almond shaped eyes where little fires glow when your heart is full. Or maybe when you squat on your heels by the low table in your room, you can sing again your hauntingly monotonous sad song, so full of yearning. Then, I think he will once more remember and cherish everything so near and dear to him. And he will take your small brown hand into his own and say to you *"Aman-siz-ba Kariss"*—"Greetings, Kariss!"

Author in 1926 with her Father, Volodymyr, and Mother, Daria

1928 at a Plast Scout camp

Author in 1930

In equestrian garb, 1930

Author at work as a journalist in 1930's

Author in Lviv 1938

Photo from Kazakhstan, early 1940's

In Kazakhstan village the author with her brother, Ihor, 1942

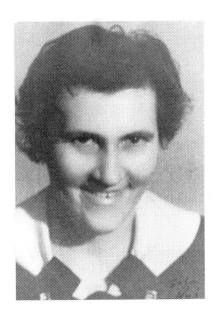

The Author in early 1950's

Photograph of the tree that grew over Juliana's mother's grave, taken by author in Kazakhstan in the 1960's

*Author, soon after her arrival to New York
City, the United States, ca 1965.*

The author in 1990's

Preparing her notes for a program in Chicago, 1993

At the Warsaw Airport in1994 with M. Chmilewsky-Ulanowicz, translator of this book

Palm (Willow) Sunday 1993, New York City

90ᵗʰ Birthday Jubilee

Original Cover

Chapter 15:

Justice

Once while visiting Washington, I somehow, unexpectedly found myself touring the Supreme Court Building with its broad white steps leading up to two rows of impressive columns, the main hall, the many corridors, the marble, and the service personnel courteously informing and directing visitors; all in all, a solemn and somber environment. As it happened, the Supreme Court was in session and, almost unawares, we found ourselves being ushered into the hearing room.

The chamber was nearly full but a respectful and attentive hush reigned. An attorney was addressing the court. Sitting behind the bench, the Supreme Court Justices, lost in concentration, rocked in their comfortable chairs from time to time. Clerks moved silently, in and out, handing the judges notes and filling their water glasses. They appeared and disappeared behind the curtain that separated the bench from the corridors. As I observed the scene, I succumbed to the atmosphere of the room and the building. It may not have been covered with the same dust of ages or the patina of tradition as some of the courts of old Europe but it was, nonetheless, stately and dignified.

Then, unexpectedly, as if on a movie screen, a different hall appeared before my eyes. In my thoughts I was transported to the past—more than ten years and many miles to the east and to the west of Washington, almost exactly to the other side of the globe.

The place was a county seat in Northern Kazakhstan. It was October—the beginning of winter—and the first snow had fallen.

The People's Court was in session. Seated on a stage-like dais the Kazakh judge was wearing a dog-skin pelt, fur-side out. On his head, the ear-flapped cap was pulled a little away from his forehead. Two women jurors sat beside him, clad in kerchiefs and padded jackets. Off a bit to the side was the prosecutor, also dressed in a pelt jacket, fur-side out. The hall was dimly lit with smoldering lamps that had been improvised from kerosene-filled bottles with twisted cotton wads stuffed through their necks for wicks.

There were several cases on the docket. I was to be a witness in the third case on the list. I sat in the audience until it was my turn and as I drew my coat around me to keep warm, I listened.

The first case had to do with a young woman who was accused of theft. She had lived in the house of a relatively well-to-do peasant, carefully noting where the owner stored her clothing and other valuables (such as they were, in that Kazakh reality). Finally, one day when the landlady was away, the girl took everything away. The judge and the two jurors listened to the testimony of the plaintiff. Sobbing, she struggled to describe in detail what had happened, how generous she had been to her tenant, how valuable the items were that were stolen, how hard she had to work for them, and the cunning treachery of the defendant.

The girl confessed to her crime. Obviously, this was not her first theft. The prosecutor spoke briefly and then the three-member court put their heads together and conferred in whispers. The verdict was announced: six months in prison.

In the middle of this trial, just as the plaintiff was enumerating all the goods that were taken from her, the door to the courtroom flew open. A freezing wind blew in. A snow-covered militiaman appeared in the doorway. Loudly, and with no regard for the trial in progress, he began shouting a name. A woman, seated in the audience, with a militiaman on either side of her, answered. Apparently she was awaiting her own trial.

"Return the shoes!" shouted the militiaman. "We're transporting the girl whose shoes you borrowed to another prison. She needs those shoes now."

"But how will I walk in the snow? Wait a bit, my trial is coming up soon. At least let me wear them back to prison." the woman begged.

"*Nichevo*, it doesn't matter. You can run barefoot over the snow. It's not that cold outside," the militiaman insisted.

And the poor woman, willy-nilly, had to take off her shoes. She passed them over the heads of the people assembled in the hall. The militiaman took them and left. Once more, the opened doors blew in snowflakes and a draft of freezing air.

This incident interrupted the testimony of the plaintiff for only a brief moment. The judge had reacted to it merely by pushing his cap further back from his forehead—as if lost in thought—and serenely observed the scene without the slightest bit of astonishment. The trial continued.

The next court case began when a Chechen woman took her place in the prisoner's dock. I knew her by sight. She and her husband, like all the other Chechens, had been deported here from the Caucasus. Her husband's, Akhmed's, workplace was near mine. I saw them often as they walked to work; he always walked ahead of her, and she, following Muslim custom, several paces behind, her eyes modestly downcast. I had paid attention to them not only because they constituted such a typically Chechen couple, but also because she was remarkably beautiful. Her large dark almond-shaped eyes were hidden behind thick and long lashes. Her thick chestnut hair was braided into a heavy knot that rested on the back of her neck. Her olive complexion brought out her fine facial features. It was evident that even though he strode ahead so confidently, and she so meekly, like a slave, several steps behind and only occasionally daring to look up at the world around her, he was very proud of the fact that he had such a beautiful wife. That is how I had seen them up to now.

Now she looked sallow and thin. Her frightened gaze shifted from judge to jury to prosecutor and then downward again. By chance, I happened to know why she was being tried.

Late in the fall, she and two other women went out into the *kolhosp* potato field. They were going to glean the leavings from the harvest. This was illegal, even though otherwise the potatoes would rot in the ground where they lay. The women managed to gather 30 kilograms. Their presence in the field had not been noticed and they quietly returned to the village. It was at this point that the village watchman, riding on horseback down the main street, saw them. He was, apparently, on his way to check on the fields. He probably would not have paid any attention to the women by the time they were in the village if they had not panicked at the sight of him; they dropped their sacks and fled. Only the Chechen, who didn't understand what was happening, did not run. She stood frozen in place. So the watchman took her and all the potato sacks to the police. Now, she was being tried for theft of all thirty kilograms.

The Chechen woman spoke no Russian and no one had bothered to translate the charges being brought against her. The court interpreter spoke to her in a very few and short sentences, which I could not understand. Maybe he was giving her a very brief version of the indictment.

Next, the watchman gave his testimony. He told the court that, as he was preparing to ride out into the fields, there, in the middle of the village, he noticed the three women walking down the street—and that they suddenly began to run as soon as they saw him. The accused Chechen woman gave a lengthy testimony that the court interpreter rendered into one short statement: "she pleads innocent, and that's all."

Again, the three heads huddled together for a brief whispered consult. The sentence: two years in prison for theft of community property. It seemed to me that the woman still did not understand what the trial was all about, what had happened to her or what lay in store for her.

The third court case had to do with my work. I was one of the witnesses but throughout my testimony, I couldn't help but think of that poor Chechen woman and compare in my mind the two "thefts" and the two sentences.

My thoughts were interrupted by a shuffling of feet that returned me to the present. The proceedings before the Supreme Court in Washington had ended. The Court issued its opinion: due to a technicality, the case against a citizen who had attempted to defraud the government of a huge amount of tax money was dismissed.

We walked out onto the marble steps that stretched downward in long, white, graceful tiers. It was only then, as I made the long descent, and seeing the Capitol and the surrounding autumn-bared rows of trees I remembered the epilogue to the case of the Chechen woman.

It was a year, maybe more, after her court case when one day, at noon, I saw Akhmed squatting "Turkish-style" with his legs crossed, leaning against the wall of the building in which he worked, as he prepared to eat his midday meal. Coming down the road, a pitiful figure, dressed in rags, approached us. It was our Chechen woman. We observed how hesitantly she drew near to her husband. Without saying a single word she crouched down on her haunches several feet away from him. Akhmed pretended not to notice her—but perhaps he did slow his hand a bit in raising his food to his mouth. This continued for a while. Finally, Petro, one of my co-workers couldn't stand it any longer. He walked up to this strange couple and, with a nod of his head in the woman's direction, said, "Well, Akhmed, it looks like you've lived long enough to see your wife come home."

Akhmed turned to Petro and, with his hand motioning towards his wife, he said, in his broken Russian, "She all bad," (that is to say, "she's worthless").

Petro tried to convince Akhmed that although thin and worn now, with some nourishment, his wife could be brought back to her old self and all would be well again. Akhmed listened in silence until finally, he held out the bowl of milk that he had been drinking from to the woman. By this gesture, he seemed to indicate that he would take her back again.

After that, we could see him walking to work, with the emaciated figure of his wife, her head bent low, again trailing some distance behind him.

Chapter 16:

Thou Shalt Not Steal

Once more, I was dreaming that I was back home. In my dream I saw a window, open wide, overlooking the trees of Yezuyitsky Park, their leaves autumn- gilt. Actually, they were never that way in real life. But in my dream, they were a brilliant golden-yellow, not rust colored, not red. A sea of golden leaves, made translucent by the sun—and then, a rain covering all this—a fine golden mist drenching the golden trees. What a good sweet dream that was!

Suddenly the rain increased, the raindrops thickened, they grew heavy. Harder and harder, like hail, they pelted the panes of the open window.

I awoke. Someone was knocking on my window. Someone's fingers were tapping lightly, persistently. I drew the curtain of the window over my bed and saw someone standing outside. Fear, our constant companion—ever present and dozing deep in our subconscious, never abandoning us—immediately rose to the surface and grabbed me by the throat.

The dark figure looming against the black of the night outside, had noticed the drawn curtain and began to speak aloud—but not too loud — directly into the window, obviously trying to avoid the attention of neighbors.

"It's us, the girls from Kurukchar. Open up!"

My fear rushed back to its normal hiding place, somewhere in the depths of my heart and brain. I rose quickly, threw on a coat and went out. In the hallway I ran into the frightened whispers of Kariss, my neighbor. She, too, must have heard the tapping on the window.

"Who is it?"

"It's alright, Kariss. It's just some friends, coming to see me."

When I opened the door, I saw not one but two figures—two young women. Outside in the pitch dark, the autumn wind was biting. A few days ago I met them—actually only one of them—while I was walking in the village. They were accompanying a transport of ox-drawn wagons from Kurukchar to the train depot.

There were many such convoys passing through our village lately. Sometimes the wagons were drawn by camels that occasionally emitted the strangest sound—something between a squeal and a roar. It seemed to me that no living creature, only a wooden or metallic machine, could possibly make such a noise. When I first heard the sound, it frightened me; but now I was no longer afraid. Some of the wagons were drawn by slow-moving oxen; they swayed their huge heads from side to side, evenly and steadily as they moved across the steppe. Some wagons were drawn by horses. These made their way more quickly to the train station. Occasionally, a larger and more prosperous *kolhosp* could afford to have a truck transport its goods. All headed to the same grain collection depot by the rail station.

The harvest had ended and the *kolhosps* had to turn over their set quotas of grain to the government. Would there be anything left over for the farm workers? The problem lay in that not only this year's quota had to be turned in, but in almost every instance the *kolhosps* owed the government part of their quotas for years past. All it took was one dry summer to put them in debt. And as droughts occurred regularly, the debt kept growing, as did the kolhosps' obligations. Unless the total grain harvest for the entire region reached the planned levels, no grain was allowed to be sold to local buyers. There was, of course, no bread allotment—unless it was for those collective farm workers who were directly involved in bringing in the harvest.

So what about everybody else? The rest of us, I suppose, would have to stop eating for the next few months—or maybe for more than just for the next few months. Would there be enough flour for bread this winter?

This cold autumn wind was a reminder that winter was very near. What would we eat? How could we stock up on provisions?

Recently, walking down the street in the village, I met this girl. She was looking around warily, holding a switch in her hand. She came up to me and, still looking over her shoulder, quietly asked me if I would be interested in buying some grain in exchange for clothing. She had immediately recognized that I was a deportee and therefore someone who might have something to trade. I knew—actually, I didn't know, I guessed—that the grain she wanted to barter was stolen from the *kolhosp*. I also knew that the penalty was a matter of many years in prison, maybe decades. On the other hand, without the wheat, the end was bound to come anyway; I would starve.

I showed the girl where I lived. We agreed that the next time she was assigned to accompany a transport of grain, she would stop by and maybe we could arrange a trade.

"But do not tell anyone about this. You understand…" she said.

Before her arrival, I had time to think about what I could exchange when she came again. There was almost nothing left of the things we brought with us. Looking at the remnants my eyes came to rest on a quilt. So far no one else wanted to buy it, and judging by its present appearance I knew I wouldn't be able sell it. But I needed something for the girls if they ever came. The comforter was quickly transformed. I carefully ripped the seams apart and it yielded three separate pieces of cloth. The rose-colored satin base, after it was washed and pressed (with an iron heated over a *kyziak* fire), looked very good and could easily pass as material for a dress; the pink damask top could serve for blouse fabric and the woolen fill could be spun into yarn suitable for knitting. Here it was—the "merchandise,"—good enough for commerce. In addition, I found some colored thread that we had received from Lviv when mailed parcels were still permitted.

There was one part of the bargain that I could not keep. Of course, I had to be very cautious about the neighbors. Each neighbor was a potential enemy who paid careful attention to our comings and goings and what we carried home. They all spied on our movements because they all were hungry and they all wanted to know where food was available. For this, they were willing to betray anybody to the authorities. That would have meant the end for me and for the girls. Still, I had to tell Kariss. Not only she, but also her children were going hungry. So I told her, but I did not give any details. I only said, "Maybe, maybe… some person might come to barter some wheat grain."

Kariss was most afraid of our neighbor Balakhanum. This woman saw and heard everything. Each time she came into our house she would scour the room with her slanty eyes, and whatever you had hidden, no matter how vigilant you were in hiding it, it would somehow always reappear and she would see it.

Every morning Balakhanum would go outside, and look around the neighborhood to see whose house already had smoke coming out of its chimney. Then she'd take a handful of straw and a tin and go begging fire. No one had matches so this kind of borrowing of fire was normal practice. Courtesy demanded, however, that one would take out only a tiny bit of the glowing *kyziak*, cover it with the straw, quickly carry it home and shove it into one's own stove. Whenever Balakhanum would borrow fire, you could be sure that she would scoop out half of all the coals in your stove so that there would barely be an ember left and you would have to add fresh *kyziak*, which was worth its weight in gold, just to cook your meal. That was Balakhanum for you and we were all a little afraid of her. So when I let the girls in, I looked around to see if anyone was nearby or if our neighbor had heard the knocking on the window. It almost seemed to me that Balakhanum was capable of hearing grass grow.

But no one was around—and the girls came inside.

Even before lighting our kerosene bottle-lantern I made certain that the window curtain was carefully drawn. The girls stood near the doorway, one of them as before, with a whip in her hand, both of them wearing quilted jackets and head kerchiefs. I asked them to sit down—and we began our bargaining.

First of all, I told them about my neighbor, Kariss. Would they be willing to trade with her? They were not too pleased. A "local" was unreliable. She might report them. But I argued that she did not even know which *kolhosp* they came from; after they left, no trace of their presence here would remain. Finally, they agreed, but first they insisted that we complete their deal with me—and then they would talk with Kariss.

I pulled out an old blouse and some other things, but they were all too worn and the girls didn't like them. Finally, the satin comforter lining caught their attention. Their eyes shone as they held it up to their faces—what a beautiful dress this would make! They also wanted the thread, and the other little notions. Now—how much wheat would I get in return for these, and where was it?

Their campsite was on the outskirts of the village, by the cemetery. The wheat would need to be carried on foot, but first we had to come to an agreement of terms. A bucket of grain was to be the unit of measure. The bargaining process was tough, with a lot of give and take. Finally, they agreed to give me six buckets of wheat and a pitcher of kerosene for all of my "merchandise."

Then I knocked on the wall to Kariss. She came bringing a bedspread and some other items from her chest. Again a spate of bargaining—and again an agreement was reached. Now came the hardest part—carrying the wheat. We decided that I would go with the girls and Kariss would stay to keep watch at home and open the door for us. She had to be careful not to let anyone in—especially Balakhanum—who, no matter how late the hour, may have seen our light and could decide to come. So, just to be sure, we extinguished the lamp and left.

A blustery wind was blowing. I was wearing a pale colored coat and I felt that everyone in the village—indeed, everyone out on the steppe—could see me. The wind was blowing my coat open because it only had one button at the top (that was the fashion back then). It was cold, but walking into the wind and holding down the sides of my coat, it wasn't too bad. I didn't have an actual grain sack, so I took an old pillow case instead.

Just as the girls had said, their campsite was beyond the village, near the cemetery. This was a path I knew well. Every day after work I would stop by my mother's grave there, under the solitary tree. So now I walked quickly down Stepova Street with its oddly scattered houses. The girls followed behind me.

The wagons were arranged in a square, as in the days when the Kirghiz nomads roamed the steppe—or maybe the way Genghis Khan himself did it. The oxen were grazing nearby. Their massive silhouettes loomed like phantoms against the dark of night. The cemetery's lone tree murmured and swayed in the wind.

No one was guarding the wagons. Maybe that was a coincidence or maybe it was by tacit agreement with the other teamsters. Like ghostly figures, we approached the wagons. I handed the pillowcase sack to the girls, and they filled it with their bare hands. The grain made a rustling sound as it streamed into the sack, making it swell, filling it. The sound of the grain blended in with the murmur of the tree, and the fitful wind's hum on the telegraph wires played an ostinato accompaniment.

The girls hoisted the sack onto my back. Completely bent over under its weight, I felt that I would break in two. But I had to carry it. I had to, because this meant life. And not mine alone!

Before setting off, I leaned the sack against a wagon and we planned a return route with the girls. Carrying the wheat was risky, so each of us had to go a separate way.

There was no moon that night. The houses in the village appeared as dark blotches and, between them, the road was just barely more visible. Further up in the center of the village, I could see its only electric lights; the mining association office and the police department were located there.

I started out. The wind was blowing my coat open—the one-button style had not foreseen this kind of expedition. I couldn't keep the sides of the coat together because now I was using both hands to hold the sack. My back felt warm—that was the wheat. I felt more conspicuous than ever. Loaded down with this dangerous cargo, and with my light colored coat flaps waving around in the wind, I was visible for miles in the open steppe. If I could just reach the nearest houses! There the wind would subside, because although the houses were spaced far apart, still they served as a windbreak. On the other hand, once there—it seemed to me— there was always someone around every corner, looking out every window, waiting to step outside and come upon me. My heart was pounding. Was it because of the weight of the sack or was it fear? I knew I had to take the shortest route, otherwise I would never make it. I simply would not have the strength. But the shortest route from the cemetery took me past the state prosecutor's house. I just saw him earlier that day. He was a Kazakh, a tall, scowling man who, as he passed by, would look somewhere over the top of my head or maybe through me.

I wondered if he had a dog.

Like lightning bolts, these thoughts kept coming at me and my heart seemed to beat somewhere up in my ears. Then I heard a sound behind me. It was a sound like that of the misty rain in my dream, rustling like a brook's tiniest whisper.

There was a hole in my pillowcase! Grains of wheat were spilling out. Not only was I sorry to lose the wheat but it was leaving a trail! It led directly to the prosecutor's doorstep and from there it would lead to my house. I grew faint. I forced myself to think as quickly, sharply, and as purposefully as I could. I could not put the sack on the ground because I knew I would never be able to pick it up again. Carrying it was one thing, but lifting it off the ground and onto my shoulder was a different matter altogether. I looked around. An empty wagon stood directly in front of the prosecutor's house. I leaned the sack against the wagon sideways so that the ripped end would be on top. Suddenly there was a clatter at the prosecutor's door. I froze. Then something slammed, again! I breathed in relief. Like all Kazakh houses, the procurator's home had a stable attached to the entrance way; it must have been the cows.

Now I had to move quickly. The pillowcase had split on the corner. I had to move the wheat around so as to tie a knot in it. My hands shook from exhaustion—or maybe from haste. The corner kept moving, slipping around, refusing to be tied. Finally… somehow…I did it.

I crouched down, I shoved the sack up onto my back and, bent in two, I continued. The sack was leaning unevenly on my back but it wasn't far now. Just a little more! I still had to pass Balakhanum's house and then I would reach my destination! The door opened as soon as I came near. Kariss, peering through cracks in the door, had been waiting for me and the girls. Drenched in sweat and, at the same time, chilled from the cold, I dragged the sack in. Once in the entranceway, Kariss helped me lift and carry it into my room.

The girls still had not arrived. I told Kariss about my adventure with the hole in the sack. Her tan face blanched in fear. What would have happened if I hadn't noticed!

Where were those girls? They should have arrived by now. We went to wait for them by the doorway. Finally two dark, hunched-over figures approached—but not from the expected direction. They were delayed because they had gotten lost—not hard to do on Stepova Street; all the houses look alike there.

Inside, we covered the windows tightly and set the kerosene bottle-lamp on the stove. Kariss brought a dry pail to measure the wheat.

Pushing the table off to one side, we put a blanket on the floor and poured the wheat onto it. A fine little pile of golden grain arose—one for me and then another for Kariss.

We listened intently for any noise, but we only heard the wild wind howling. Sometimes our hearts skipped a beat if it seemed to knock on the windows or bang on the rickety door.

Finally, our transaction was complete. We let the girls out and they disappeared amid the houses into the night's gloom. It was only then that I noticed that they took with them some things that we hadn't bargained for.... But we had our wheat. Starvation was staved off temporarily.

We hid our acquisition. I went to bed feeling tired, but strangely awake. I couldn't sleep. My back ached. Inside my head, thoughts jumped around from one thing to another.

Suddenly it occurred to me that I—yes, I—had just taken part in a theft. Well, maybe only indirectly. But what did my conscience, that finely tuned compass that differentiates between what is allowable and what is not, have to say about it? Had it really gathered so much rust that it no longer functioned? Not so long ago, even as Poland was collapsing, my conscience decided that things that had been left behind and thus no longer belonged to anybody were still untouchable. Was this moral decline the inevitable result of war and lawlessness? Because I didn't experience the slightest bit of remorse now, only exhaustion and the memory of paralyzing fear—especially the fear I felt near the prosecutor's house.

And then a new thought struck me like lightning. The tiny rivulet of grain had ended precisely at the procurator's house! Any theft would be traced to him!

I laughed silently. I think that when I finally fell asleep, I fell asleep with a smile on my face.

My dream of the trees with their golden leaves and the golden rain in Yezuyitskiy Park didn't come back. Instead, I dreamed of the prosecutor—just as I had seen him—the tall and scowling Kazakh, who in passing, never looked directly at me, only over or through me. This time, in my dream, he was wearing his winter garb, a dog-pelt jacket, fur-side out. Maybe it came from the dog who should have been keeping guard outside his house last night.

Chapter 17:

A Happy Man's Shirt

The shirt of a truly happy man is said to have the power to restore health to an ailing caliph.

But there was only one man in the whole country, a shepherd, who claimed to be truly happy, and he was shirtless.

A folk tale

An old, no longer operative dairy building was going to be the site of the New Year's Eve party. All the kolhosp workers, with their families in tow, were in a hurry to arrive. Party or no party, New Year or no New Year, there was only one thing that really mattered: food was going to be served. They kept coming and coming, trampling a deep and narrow path in the recently fallen snow.

There was a potbellied cast-iron stove in the middle of the shop floor. Neatly arranged bricks of the best sheep manure patties were already burning inside. The stove door began to take on a distinctly rosy hue. Nonetheless, the walls inside the building remained covered with frost.

As people entered, they shook off the snow from their *valianky* and brushed them off with a whisk. Then, without removing their outer clothing, they all searched for a seat at one of the tables. First, the area immediately around the stove was taken, then wherever there was still room. The plant manager and the other bosses, all "free" men, were seated at the table nearest the center of the room. Farther away from the middle were the laborers. They were mostly "*natsmeny*"[15]: the locals (Kazakhs and other Kazakhstani natives) and the deportees. They sat in clusters: some Azeris here, some Ukrainians there, a group of Poles, a group of Volga Germans. In the farthest corner, a group of Chechens had wound themselves into a tight knot. They alone had come without their wives. Not because their wives weren't hungry, but because that was part of their tradition, a part of their unwritten law.

The weak light produced by the "soot-maker" lanterns alternated between casting eerie shadows on the walls or making the frosty crystals glisten like New Year's decorations.

The tables were set with platters of *pyrizhky*—baked dumplings stuffed with carrots or defrosted sugar beets. Before long, bowls of a hot broth with meat appeared. Everyone was tempted by the aroma but no one dared to start eating.

Those seated at the head table talked loudly, breaking into frequent laughter, slapping each other on backs and knees, and ignoring the fact that everyone else was just waiting to delve into the hot soup, hunt down their piece of meat and quickly follow it up with a *pyrizhok*. The workers cast furtive sideway glances, their eyes darting from food to plant manager and back again. Finally he seemed to get the point.

"Alright, let's go at it! While it's hot!" And he himself began to eat.

Like a wind sweeping through the hall, everyone stirred. People roused themselves and began to eat. They ate slowly at first, cautiously, seemingly embarrassed by their hunger and trying to hide it. A few moments of discreet nibbling were followed by subdued murmurs of conversation, and finally that gave way to a general roar.

Ushaty, huge dairy canisters, laden with fermented whey-beer, were brought in. Tin measuring cups, also belonging to the dairy, were filled and passed from hand to hand. As food and beer gradually loosened tongues, noise and hubbub filled the hall. The director, having finished with his food, was forced to clap his hands and bang a metal cup

---

15 *natsmeny*= a pejorative term in Russian for non-Russians (from "national minority").

in order to quiet the noisy crowd. Then he delivered something that vaguely resembled a New Year's address; it was full of all the familiar and trite phrases about the Happy Soviet Man, the Motherland and the Party. Finally, he shouted: "An accordion. Come on! Let's get an accordion up here!"

The head table was pushed back and everyone squeezed in even more tightly. A circle of open space appeared on the clay floor around the stove. The musician took his place. He struck a few chords as if testing the instrument and the agility of his fingers. Then he began to play. "Katiusha" was followed by "Metelytsia" and, then, some other songs. Some people were still eating; others sang along quietly or swayed in time to the music. Finally, after a melancholy "Suliko," the accordionist, without a break, began playing *chastushky*—Russian dance ditties. At that point, some people began to tap their feet in time to the music, and before long they were ready to dance. The manager began by taking a few mincing *chastushka* steps himself. He called out, first to his cronies then to those in the other groups, to join him in dance.

Perhaps it was the beer, or maybe something even stronger, that made him increasingly merrier, whooping aloud and singing along. Shoving his cap back to the top of his head and removing his shearling jacket, he called out in time to the music,

"Come on, come on! Everybody dance! We'll all have fun together!" Then, looking toward the group of the deported "westerners," he added, "Not like those... bourgeoisie!"

The earflaps of his cap jumped in time to his movements, its shadow on the wall resembling some fanciful bird. Occasionally one of the laborers would walk out to the center of the floor and attempt to ape the manager's merriment by hopping around as best he knew.

The stove, the dancing and the beer warmed everyone. The air became heavy with the thick smell of steamy clothing and *valianky*, the soot of the lanterns and the smoke of the burning *kyziak*. Some took off their quilted or sheepskin jackets.

Only the group of Chechens stood apart, close to one another, compressed into the darkest corner of the hall. In their tall and wide-at-the-top, black lambskin hats they looked like towering demi-giants. The dancing manager noticed that they were standing quietly, off by themselves, and with a hand motion tried to call one of them out onto the dance floor. Instead, they closed in together even more tightly.

Then the boss pushed his way out to them, and grabbing the nearest one, he pulled him out onto the dance floor. The Chechen resisted, but as soon as he found himself out in the middle he quickly caught on to the beat, and imitating the boss, he managed to stomp out a rather lively *chastushka*.

"Why you so-and-so! Look how well he dances!" shouted the manager, shoving back his cap, which kept falling in his face. "Now, how about smiling? You look like you're dancing at a wake!"

It was getting hotter and hotter, especially for those dancing by the stove. The manager and others had shed their outer garments, their padded jackets and their shearling coats, long ago. Still, rivulets of perspiration poured out from under their caps. The Chechen's forehead, too, glistened with sweat. His face had turned quite red.

"Take off your jacket!" commanded the director.

The Chechen didn't seem to hear or understand. He continued hopping around in time to the beat.

"Take it off, I say. What's wrong, can't you hear me?" shouted the manager encouragingly. But the Chechen did not take it off; instead he drew the belted government-issue jacket even more tightly around him.

"Will you take it off or not?" the boss's voice had a hard edge to it now.

At that point, the Chechen stopped and looked toward his countrymen. They were whispering among themselves. The director refused to give up. He grabbed the Chechen by the arm before he could make his way through the crowd.

"Who do you think you are? Everybody else is having a good time, so what's wrong with you? You don't like it? What makes you think you're so much better than anyone else? You don't even know how well off you are! Take off your jacket, I'm telling you, and get back to dancing!"

Someone else had decided to help hold down the stubborn Chechen. The director laughed and cursed as he unbelted him and started to undo the buttons. Suddenly he stopped, letting out a string of obscenities, and released the Chechen, who rewrapped himself tightly into his government-issue jacket and quickly pushed back into his group of friends.

The manager stood there dumbfounded. Mechanically, out of sheer force of habit, he was still hurling curses, but the alcohol seemed to have evaporated from his brain. He stared wide-eyed at the Chechens, then shrugging in disgust, he sat down on the closest bench.

Still, no one there knew what exactly had happened. Only the manager and the man who stood next to him saw that beneath the Chechen's government-issue jacket there was nothing but bare flesh. He was shirtless.

Chapter 18:

Somewhere, Spring Was Coming!

One day you find yourself standing and looking out of the doorway of your house. Everything appears to be the same as always: the same haphazardly arranged neighboring houses with their flat roofs, each one with snow reaching up to the eaves (or, at least, up to the windows), each with its own mound of manure that had been pitched out of the adjoining stable and saved over the winter season. (*Kiziak* as fuel was precious).

But now, each manure pile was sweating and a steamy cloud hovered above each one. This was a sign, a sign that spring was on its way.

Another sign of spring was the snow; it just wasn't the same. For the uninitiated, for the newly arrived in Kazakhstan, the change was imperceptible, but I knew. I learned years ago. This was a different kind of snow.

It happened, I think, the first year that we were here, about this same time of the year. Someone was always needed to go fetch water. The well was not close by, almost a kilometer away. It was hard work. Later I had to do it all by myself because I lived alone and my brother had been sent far away, but at first I didn't worry about it too much because he was the one who would carry the water.

It wasn't easy because water dripped from the buckets, then froze and made the path slippery. Drawing the water was even harder. The normally low rim of the well (the only one in the entire village) was covered with a thick wall of ice leaving only a very small opening to the well, barely large enough for the bucket to pass through. The trick was to keep your balance as you stood on the mountain of ice in front of the well and manipulated the hooked pole to which the bucket was attached.

You had to fill the bucket without losing it in the well, because—where would you get another one? You would pour the drawn water into a second bucket, and then let the first bucket down to be filled again. If you had a yoke (and knew how to use it) you had to attach the two full buckets to the yoke and then place it on your shoulders. This wasn't as easy as it might seem, especially with the straight rods that the Kazakhs used as yokes. If you didn't know how to manipulate these, you just had to carry the buckets in your hands.

One time my brother got sick. His arm was swollen from an anti-typhoid fever vaccine and he couldn't carry anything. So we went together. He would help draw the water and I would carry it. My brother walked along the well-trod path but I decided that I wanted to take a shortcut. I took just a few steps before sinking into waist-deep snow. I tried lifting a leg but the *valianka* was stuck firmly in the snow and I pulled up a bare foot. The more I struggled, the deeper I sank. My brother stood there on the path and made fun of me for trying to outsmart him. He laughed for a while and then he went to look for a shovel. He threw it to me and I had to dig through the heavy wet snow until I finally got to the firm tamped-down path. If I had been there by myself, it could have ended badly.

I heard once that a horse almost "drowned" in the snow on a neighboring street. Another time people saw some horns sticking out of the snow and dug out a cow that had wandered into a snowdrift, got buried and died there.

So now I knew. This was a different kind of snow. Although still white, it had a bluish tint to it and it had become glisteningly smooth. It was losing its crispness. It didn't even squeak underfoot in the same way.

So, a different kind of snow was the second sign that spring was on its way.

The third sign of approaching spring were my *valianky,* my felt boots. All winter, though old and patched, they kept my feet warm. All I had to do was diligently brush the snow off them as soon as I came home. That's why every house and office had a special twig broom to keep the snow from melting and penetrating the felt, and thereby robbing the boots of their ability to retain warmth. The boots had to be dried out overnight on top of the stove. But now they no longer kept me warm. They were absorbing so much wet snow out on the street that it was impossible to dry them completely over the barely warm stove.

So here are the three main indications of spring in Kazakhstan:

1. Steam rising off the manure mounds.
2. Snow losing its crispness.
3. Valianky losing their warming ability (even when they have no holes).

There was a calendar on the office wall. It confirmed that spring had arrived.

How wonderful and yet how painful it was to remember and to imagine! I could close my eyes and see. I could remember a real spring. The mist over the willows, their crowns enveloped in a yellowish-green veil, proclaiming that spring was near. The smell of earth, black and moist, ready to receive the sown seeds—this too was spring's aroma, long before any fragrant flowers appeared. The call of the migrating birds, returning home from distant southlands. How it hurt to remember all this! And still, the memories evoked hope. Maybe, once more, we would see the blossoming orchard on St George's Hill. Maybe we would gaze again at the maples as they drew a lacy edge against the blue sky in Yezuyitskiy Park.

I realized that someone was speaking to me, and I awoke from my reverie. It was Sonia—a young Ukrainian girl, born here in Kazakhstan.

"Are you alright? Didn't you hear me talking to you?" she asked.

"It's spring back home, Sonia! Soon the orchards will be in full bloom!"

"So how do orchards bloom? What does a blossoming tree look like? I've read about apple and cherry blossoms. What are they like? At least you know; you've seen them! I wonder if I ever will."

I looked at Sonia and I felt sorry for her. I wondered. Which was better: to ache for what I once knew or, like Sonia, never to know the pale pink apple blossom… never to know the glory of spring, "in flow'rs and pearls bedecked"?

Chapter 19:
The Spoils of War

First came the letters.

An elderly Uzbek, with a thick black goatee, came to us. He was also a deportee, and bending from the waist, with his hand on his heart, he brought a letter from his son, which he asked that we read to him. Whenever he saw us on the street or at the market he would bow in that characteristically dignified oriental manner. Apparently he was a mullah who was literate, but only in Uzbek script and the letter was written in Russian. He too had been deported to Kazakhstan, even though his son was in the Red Army.

As soon as we began reading the letter, our hearts stopped. His son was writing from "The Carpathians…" The mullah did not understand why reading that his son was part of a unit that was battling resistance fighters would be so difficult for us. The mullah did not know anything about these freedom fighters, who and what they were. He was only interested in knowing whether his son was alive and well. It was puzzling to him why it was hard for us to keep up a conversation.

The letters arrived from many different parts of Europe: Krakow, Katowice, even as far away as Germany. They always included something about the health of the writers and about victories in battle, but they also contained descriptions—naïve and cryptic—of Europe, that unknown and alien world. Those details struck us as most quaint. There was, for example, a description of a kitchen—unexpectedly stuck in the middle of a report of a victory and news of the writer's advancing unit. It was a simple but accurate account. To his right, the writer wrote, there was a sideboard, then there was a stove—but it wasn't made of clay with a built-in cauldron, and it was heated by gas or electricity not by manure patties or straw. Then, hanging over the windows, there were these odd-looking (to the writer) floral-patterned cloths.

Packages followed the letters. Their contents, too, were quite outlandish. Sometimes they were so strange that the recipients themselves would come and ask us to explain what these things were. One such package contained what must have been the entire decor of some typically middle class European bedroom—knick-knacks, china figurines, a painting of elks by a stream. It was obvious that the sender had looted and packed in haste everything he could find in someone's vacated (or maybe not) apartment.

What to do about these bedspreads, rugs and drapes? Against a background of dirt floors—because wood floors here were very rare—and tiny windows these things were so incongruously out of place. But it didn't take long before someone found a way of putting them to good use. They could be sewn into the most amazing clothes!

One time a young Kazakh woman came to work wearing a pink satin lace-up foundation garment over her dress. It had arrived in a package and it reminded her of laced jackets that she had seen somewhere. It was both comical and sad to see her and then her disappointment when she learned its true purpose.

Another person received a crateful of soap. He quickly sold the bars because soap was a rare commodity and highly valued by… enthusiasts of cleanliness. A letter followed explaining that wristwatches were embedded within the soap bars. Someone must have lathered up a batch of treasures for themselves.

Then there was a package of women's shoes, almost all high-heeled. Another package appeared to be theatrical costumes. Kitchen utensils, delicate shellfish forks, and cake servers, were all mixed in with a little girl's First Communion dress—probably a treasured heirloom— and ball gowns. I wondered who danced in those lacy gowns and what was the occasion? Was it, maybe, some girl's first dance—or perhaps her last? Was she beautiful? Was she kind or cruel? Maybe, wearing the dress, she bid farewell to a German youth as he was leaving to wage war in the East?

Our village was built on a grid, like New York City: a few very long and very broad streets interspersed by narrow alleys. Open steppe filled the spaces between the streets and the alleys. One time I saw a strange figure, clad entirely in black, walking down one of these. It was such an odd sight that I could not suppress my curiosity. I noticed that others were also stopping and staring. I cut across one of the open fields to catch up with this tottering and slow moving dark figure. As I neared him, I could make out a wide-brimmed black hat with a rounded crown and an ankle-length outer garment. As I came closer, a silhouette of a Protestant pastor came into focus. Only his gait somehow did not fit, and what, O Lord, would a pastor be doing here anyway? Finally, I stood face to face with "the pastor" and I saw the slanted eyes, the high cheekbones, the flattened nose and the scant little beard. There, you have the pastor! That gait had been familiar because that is how Kazakhs walk— in short, slightly wobbly steps.

After the letters and then packages came the returning soldiers. First, it was the invalids and those who had been wounded. They too, brought with them anything they could carry away. It sometimes happened that if a returnee could not find his own family, he would move into any house at the edge of the village. After all, who wouldn't take in such a "rich" person? Then, he would move from one house to another until, finally settling down, he found some woman worthy of becoming his wife.

One day I was at the railroad station, waiting for a train. As it happened, I had to wait several days. On any given day there was only one train going in the direction where I was headed. If the train was full, no more tickets would be sold and one would have to wait around for the next train to arrive on the following day. Therefore we camped out at the station—outside during the day, inside the waiting area (if they let us) at night. Occasionally, someone living nearby would let us sleep on the floor in their house. It was fall but it was not cold yet. A group of us waited together. The wait might have been a welcome respite from work if it were not for the worry that time was passing and I still didn't have a ticket. Still, there was a lot to see.

For example, a special train, part freight and part passenger came by. One of the platform cars was loaded with leather club chairs. Sprawled out on one of these was a returning veteran with his feet up on the armrest, an accordion next to him. Of course, there were many bicycles, and occasionally a motorcycle or two. There was an elegant decorated veneer bedroom suite with two beds. Soldiers were sprawled out on them, smoking and warming themselves in the autumn sun. Another sat on a Bidermayer sofa, playing an accordion. And still another, wearing a silk top hat, was tipping it and bowing to the people at the station.

The train stopped and the soldiers disembarked to eat at the station restaurant reserved especially for them. Some soldiers who came from the nearby villages recognized people they knew among those waiting at the station and eagerly asked about their families. Occasionally that led to heartbreaking moments when they learned that their families were gone. They went away somewhere. Where did they go? The Soviet Union was so huge!

I overheard soldiers talking about their experiences and their deeds (all heroic, of course—that's true of all homecoming war stories). There was a young boy with a leg wound—obviously causing him pain— standing not too far from me. He was surrounded by older women; he probably reminded them of their own sons. There was a sadness to his story.

"Here there was this one time," he said, "when we walked into the post office and found these packages intended for the German army! We opened one and it contained some useful things, so we took them. But, then, we thought, 'maybe the others packages have something even better in them.' So we'd rip apart more. It was impossible to take everything! But by then some kind of frenzy would come upon us. If we couldn't take anymore we'd just break them all apart. Later, I was kinda embarrassed by our shameful behavior.... But as for the others—well... it didn't matter to them, it wasn't theirs anyway. Sometimes we'd go into a house... and bang on the piano until it would groan Then all the guys would start in, breaking up everything, throwing stuff around, tearing the place apart."

Another soldier said to him, "What's the matter with you? Are you going soft? What are you, some sort of cry baby? That's just what we were supposed to do—destroy everything! Who did you want to leave it to? The Germans?"

"The Germans were destructive," said the young boy, "but we should have behaved better."

This discussion might have continued, but it was time to go. The soldiers jumped back onto the railroad car, waved goodbye to their new friends at the station… and then they were gone. It wasn't too long before another train arrived. It was hauling more furniture: a kitchen stove, a fashionable living room suite, a new table and… a mirror. It was a huge mirror—obviously part of someone's boudoir. As it reflected the bright sun, its sculpted crystal frame broke the sunlight into a myriad of rainbows. It had been well wedged in and had survived the thousands of kilometers intact. The owner of this piece of booty got off the train to go to the restaurant. He was very proud of his new possession and he told everyone that it was a gift for his wife. He didn't have that much farther to go now—just to the next station.

The rest stop was a fairly long one so there was plenty of time for the mirror owner to socialize and talk. After an hour of making conversation, it turned out that someone there knew his wife.

"Katia Ivanova? So you're her husband? Why are you going on then? She lives right here, near this station."

"Here? Don't tell me she moved! Why?"

The question produced an uncomfortable silence, and then finally, an uncomfortable answer.

"I don't know– I guess…because."

"Well, for heaven's sake tell me why! What's going on here? Exactly where does she live now?"

The train whistle signaled a departure. The soldier jumped back into the car and began throwing down his bundles. If his wife was living here—that meant that he would have to get off here. His friends helped him unload, one package, then another. Now there was just one item left, the most important—the mirror. The train began to move away slowly from the station.

"Wait!" the soldier shouted in the direction of the locomotive. "Damn it to hell, wait!" he shouted to the signalman on duty.

The train continued to move. Very carefully, his comrades pushed the mirror to the edge of the railcar until it touched the ground. It was standing almost upright and seemed quite secure… but then… it tipped over and… BAM! With a heavy thud and a tinkling crash, all at once, it lay there in tiny fragments.

The sunlight reflected off the broken glass. The train continued to pick up speed. Some of the soldiers on the train laughed uproariously, others cursed and still others just stared silently in wide-eyed amazement. Standing over the shattered mirror, its owner was struck speechless. It had survived so many miles—only for this to happen! At first he couldn't even curse, he just stood there in wordless shock.

After a minute or so his lips let out a string of juicy curses. Finally, shrugging in disgust, he began to gather his other belongings and then he left, in search of his wife.

The shattered crystalline shards of mirror lay there at the railroad station. Part of some distant salon, hallway, or parlor the mirror had traveled all those miles just to arrive here and break into a thousand shining little rainbow pieces. Its story, however, had not yet ended. A group of young Kazakh girls appeared and began gathering the larger fragments. They were big enough to reflect the girls' dark almond-shaped eyes, their triangular tan faces and their little snub noses. The mirror was still useful. And certainly, for some, those eyes and noses were just as attractive as the features of some European lady who peered into the mirror thousands of kilometers to the west.

Did the soldier ever find his wife? I do not know. Maybe his family, too, had shattered—like the mirror that he wanted to present to his wife.

Chapter 20:
The History of a Tunic

A meeting was going to be held in the village square. The streets that bordered the square of this regional center were where all the main government agencies were located: the NKVD,[16] the post office, the district accounting office, and the bank. There was a hitching area outside the bank where you could tie up your horse, or camel, or leave your ox cart. That space was designated for those who were arriving from distant collective farms and villages. In the middle of the square there was a church—formerly a church—now a club, a movie house and a meeting hall. Some locals who felt they could trust us more than their own fellow-villagers told us how the church had been desecrated. They said that the man who had been sent up on the roof to take down the cross, fell off. From others we heard that it was more than one man who fell off, and that each time anyone tried to climb up, he would fall off. Maybe it was true, or maybe it was just a pious legend going back to the time when a church was still considered a house of God and its cross dominated the village. Now, the damaged cross hung limply from the onion dome of the present-day "house of culture"—the club.

This village even had a few trees. Someone was trying to grow a small grove of poplars in the church square. But it's hard for poplars to grow here. Each spring, work crews from various agencies would be

---

16   NKVD= The Soviet Ministry of Internal Affairs, the predecessor of the KGB

driven out to cultivate these tress and plant more. But it was an uphill battle. In the winter, the poplars struggled against the wind and the snow. In the summer, they struggled against the wind and the drought. Throughout the year, regardless of season, they were at the mercy of livestock—the cattle, the camels, the goats and the sheep who were always breaking their branches. The village council sent workers every year to plant and dig around the trees but that was the extent of their care.

These poplars were unusual. They were fragrant. Their young spring foliage had a soft smell, a little like honey and a little like some exotic perfume. In the spring, if there was a breeze blowing from the square as you entered the village, their gentle fragrance greeted you. Crushed, the young leaves left an aromatic green sap on the palms of your hands—like a sweet-smelling green blood. In the summer, the leaves quickly darkened, and then yellowed in the burning sun, losing their fragrance.

So that's where the meeting to celebrate some victory against the Germans was going to be held. Everybody, from all the workplaces, was required to be there. Of course, the work we missed still had to be made up—on our own time, whether in the evenings or at night. In addition, I had a hard time walking because I was always waging war with my footwear. It was too warm to wear my felt boots and the flimsy straps on my sandals were always breaking and falling off my feet. So I walked barefooted. Lagging behind the rest of the crowd herded from the factory, I had decided, "If my feet start to hurt from the thorns in the road or the hot sand, then I'll put on my sandals."

And yet, I could not help but admire the poplar trees whose young, still-green leaves shimmered in the wind. They didn't seem to be part of this gray environment. It was spring, but already the sun was beginning to bear down. Some speaker was holding forth and the gathered crowd cheered—while we just waited for the meeting to come to an end. But wait—there was going to be some kind of parade! Over the shoulders of those standing around me I could see schoolchildren and members of collective farms marching past. Then, some distance away I could see Kazakhs on horseback approaching. They bounced around on their ponies in that characteristic steppe-style gallop, their elbows akimbo, flapping like wings. From afar, I saw a young Kazakh sporting a skullcap and—Good Lord!—what was that? Forcing my way rudely through the crowd, I could finally see all of him and he was wearing something that was very familiar to me. That tunic that he wore was once part of a formal ensemble of mine! Made of blue silk and bound in gold trim, it had billowing white sheer sleeves embroidered in blue and gold. As the Kazakh's elbows flapped in the wind like birds' wings, my beautiful embroidered sleeves waved in time to the horse's gait. The long loose sides of the dark blue vest also swung back and forth. I couldn't tear my eyes away from him. Obviously proud of his outfit and of his breakneck horsemanship, he galloped back and forth, showing off before the crowd.

All at once, the village square—and the grey, colorless crowd that filled it, the people in their padded vests, and the Kazakh women with their veiled heads—vanished before my eyes. I was aware only of my tunic, my dear lovely tunic!

The Kazakh on his horse—as if to spite me—kept riding back and forth right in front of me. And yet it all seemed unreal. Only the tunic was real. What I was hearing was not the rustle of the poplar trees but an orchestra playing a sentimental waltz, the last dance at the ball. As the song was being played, dawn was breaking. Couples were swirling to a steady beat. Lurking in each corner of the ballroom, young men were waiting to break in and whisk me away—off to the center of the ballroom, where no one else could cut in anymore.

My dark blue silk ensemble was composed of a slim skirt topped by the tunic, cut folk-style and trimmed in gold braid. The attached white silk sleeves were embroidered in blue and gold. A gold lamé braided headpiece, wide over the forehead and tapering toward the back, topped my black hair. Now even I (never pleased with my own appearance) had to admit that the total effect was really quite attractive. A necklace of tiny golden crosses from my grandfather's antique collection hung round my neck.

Before the ball began, there was a presentation of authentic Ukrainian regional folk dress. I modeled an outfit from the area around Tyshkovytsi. It was judged to be the most picturesque in the show and although the prize was awarded for the costume, not for me, I still basked in its glow. My aunt who was born and lived in Tyshkovytsi sent the ensemble to me; it was the outfit she had chosen for her burial.

It arrived folded in such a way as to ensure that each piece would be donned in proper order. Even the headpiece was pinned to a wooden dowel to retain its shape. And although we tried very hard to follow her instructions, my aunt still complained that we did not tie the *kraika*, the woven sash, properly. It was several yards long and it was supposed to cinch me in like a corset. Still, the costume was lovely, and the loveliest part of it all was the red crown of braided yarn.

Following the folk dress show there was a contemporary Ukrainian fashion show that utilized not only homespun textiles and country prints but also elements of folk embroidery and design. An example of this was the formal dress I wore, (created, I think, by Madam Nizhankowska).

The ball followed. It lasted until the wee hours of the morning and it did not end until, accompanied by one of the most popular dance bands of the day, the whole assembly sang the traditional and gaily sentimental last waltz.

Of course, it's hard to say just how that dress ended up among the bundles that we took with us to Kazakhstan. We had only minutes to pack our belongings and it was all done under guard. Many random items got wrapped in the Tyshkovetska-woven cloth that we yanked off the table—and many useful things were left behind.

At first we exchanged items we didn't mind parting with. However as time went on, we were willing to trade anything at all—even what we were wearing at the time of the exchange if our trading partner liked it—because we had to eat. But my mother always hid my tunic ensemble. She desperately wanted me to keep it—if only for the embroidered sleeves.

"When you return home," she would say (and this was always spoken with such absolute certitude that the unlikely seemed somehow possible), "You can sew those sleeves onto something else and you will still have them, because, you will never own anything so unique again."

When Mother became ill and we desperately sought to buy at least a tiny amount of butter for her, we discovered that not a single item of her belongings was left among our possessions. She had traded away her own things first and saved ours for later barter. Among the remaining treasures was my tunic—it lay there at the very bottom of the chest. Eventually its turn came too. By then Mother was no longer around to protect it and my brother needed to be outfitted for the "Labor Army." And I—well, I didn't care anymore. Some Kazakh woman bought it and—as I remember—even paid fairly well for it during that very hungry year. I completely forgot that I ever owned it. Until now.

I stood barefoot on the ground that was growing hotter by the minute. Before long, there would be no walking on it without burning the soles of my feet. Wearing a nondescript cotton dress and holding my sandals in my hand, I stared at the Kazakh who was grandstanding, celebrating some military victory—in my beautiful tunic.

I heard the sound of the crowd applauding the speaker and the waltz died in my ears. The hot sand bit at my feet. We started walking back to the factory and again I lagged behind everyone else, as I tried to avoid the thorns and barbs in the road. The Kazakh who was wearing my tunic quickly rode past us and disappeared onto a side street.

Chapter 21:

Smoke

Our office moved to a different location for the summer. Now I could look out from my work window and see our home among the *rozvaliushky*, the ruined and long-abandoned houses built of sun-baked clay. In time, the snow, the rain and the frigid cold had dissolved and crumbled the bricks. Someone decided to repair one of these; they plastered it with fresh clay, thatched the roof with willow branches—and lived in it for a time, but then, they too abandoned it. That was where we spent a winter.

Through an opening among the ruins, I could see the entrance to our house. Mother stayed inside most of the time. All winter she lay ill on her pallet. Now that the weather had turned warm (but before the sun became too strong), she was strong enough to rise from bed and I could see her coming out of the house, taking her stool out and sitting in the shade. She was always busy doing something and I always tried to guess what it was. Sometimes she would grind roast wheat for "coffee," or mend clothes. Occasionally it seemed that there was a book resting on her lap.

There was always a black dot next to her—that would be the little dog. The previous tenants of the *rozvaliushka* took the dog with them when they moved but the dog came back anyway. Mother said that she had never seen an uglier dog. It was short, its legs were crooked and its tail seemed to be stuck, somehow, in the wrong place. It's not hard to love a beautiful pedigreed dog. But Mother loved this one. It kept her company and it protected her; if anyone approached the house, it would start yapping long in advance.

By the time the sun reached its zenith at noon, Mother would no longer be seen sitting outside. The hot air shimmered over the flat roof. A barely visible ribbon of smoke emerged from the chimney.

When we were children we used to draw houses. We would start with a rectangle; inside that rectangle were two smaller rectangles. The smaller ones, like eyes, had crosses in them—these were the windows. Then, between them, there was third rectangle for the door. Sometimes a curved path led away from the door; it represented freedom—the freedom to walk out of and away from the house. The rectangle of the house would always be topped off by a roof and a chimney. A curly and puffy smoke would emerge from the chimney, rising either straight up into the sky or, imaginatively, off to the side. The smoke we children drew was a happy symbol, a sign of life within the house.

However, I hated the smoke that I would see coming from our chimney among the ruined hovels. I knew what it meant. In my mind's eye I could see it. At the opening to our Russian-style baker's oven there was an iron tripod atop which the cook pot would rest. Under the tripod there were always some dried weeds and *kiziak*, the dung-fuel patty. We gathered the manure from old pastures—but it was never sufficiently dry so as to burn right. The moist patty gave off an acrid, foul-smelling smoke that filled the house, and then Mother would always start coughing. Whenever I saw this wispy smoke rising from our chimney, I could almost hear her coughing in the office where I worked.

Mother would blow on the weeds and the *kiziak* to make them burn. She had to bend low over the tripod. Her hands shook from the strain until her knuckles turned white as she grasped the edge of the stove. Those dear, familiar, gentle hands! The most beautiful hands in the world! The skin was not white and the nails were not like those of some beautiful, carefully manicured women. The skin on her hands, always fragile, was now red and torn from gathering and breaking thorny weeds and shrubs. Her nails were cracked and broken. Her fingers (remember how she used to amaze us with their flexibility by bending her pinky back to touch her wrist?) were burned, scarred and stiff.

Those hands were once capable of conjuring the most wonderful music out of our cherrywood piano, music that I have cherished since childhood. Always, whenever I heard it, I could see our parlor with its piano, the portrait of my grandmother hanging over it, the china cabinet next to it along with all the rest of the family furnishings. As we listened to her play it wasn't just Chopin's Etude or Beethoven's Pathetique Sonata. For us, it was simply Mother's music.

Now she leaned against the three-legged iron stove with those same dear hands, attempting to blow some life into the fire. The fire refused to burn and so she kept blowing, coughing and blowing, until her eyes watered from the smoke.

We begged Mother not to blow, not even to try to cook if the fire wouldn't burn. But she felt she had to—it was every mother's duty to cook for her children. Our pleas and arguments were useless. Whenever we would come home at noon, there would always be something hot that she had prepared for us.

She lay in bed all winter, ill and coughing. The straw in her mattress had rotted from the moisture that came up from the dirt floor. Inside, the walls were covered with frost. Outside, the house was completely covered with snow. Only one narrow path led to the house.

Now that the weather had warmed a bit, Mother was able to rise from bed. But the smoke was still making her cough. I was filled with hatred for that smoke. Every time I saw a thin wisp rising from our chimney, I knew that most of it was filling the house and that it was choking her.

As evening drew near, I would see her sitting in front of the house again. That would be close to the time that we would be coming home from work. She always waited for us. Slowly she would pace, back and forth, back and forth. She looked so small and alone among these abandoned ruins. She waited. It seems that it was her fate in life—always to be waiting for someone. She waited for Father when he was a *striletz* during the war, then she waited when he was a prisoner of war, then again, after the war ended when he would travel on business. Finally, she had to wait for us, her children, when our life's paths took us each in our own direction. Always, she was waiting for someone, waiting and worrying. So now, still, she paced before the house and waited.

How could I protect her against her suffering, against her cough and against the loneliness of the *rozvaliushky*? What could I do to end her waiting so that finally all of us—including Father—could be together?

*   *   *   *

We received permission to move to another town. Amnesty had been declared. Our new home would be closer to the railroad station but along the same rail line to prevent any possibility of having Father's and our paths accidentally cross. Amnesty was extended to all Polish citizens regardless of ethnicity. Therefore it seemed likely that Father would be released as well.

We hoped that by leaving this village with its solitary tree, we would also leave behind Mother's illness, the hunger, the cough, the despair, the separation from Father—and the smoke.

It was a beautiful, if cold, wintery day when we moved into our "new" village. The two main streets were lined in poplars.

"Look, Mother, trees!"

But Mother was incapable of taking pleasure in the trees. The day after we moved into our new surroundings she became ill again. Maybe the trip wore her out. I hoped that by resting in bed she would revive and be up on her feet again, that she would see the trees, now adorned in white frost, and that she could look forward to Father's expected arrival on this very road that led from the train station. But she did not have the strength to get out of bed. We moved her bed near the window which looked out onto the road and the frost-covered trees. Soon she lost the strength even to sit up and look.

In addition, soon after she took ill, the smoke returned. "It's her enemy," I thought, "it followed us here."

Maybe the stove was defective, or maybe it was the *kiziak*. Although we now bought, rather than just gathered it half-wet from the pastures, still maybe someone had mixed in dirt with it, and made it useless. Maybe I just didn't know how to make it burn right. Everybody was giving us advice as to how to get rid of the smoke. I felt an immense hatred for it, as if it were some living being, some incarnation of the evil that was tormenting my mother. It seemed that in the battle for Mother's life I was struggling, not so much with Mother's illness, as with that smoke.

Crouching down before the stove, I tried to warm the house and cook a meal. But the stove's fire chamber produced no fire, only acrid smoke. Even if I did manage to get a real fire started, after I prepared the meal some smoke always remained, lurking in crevices, hiding behind Mother's cot (we banged together some borrowed boards so she would have her own place to sleep instead of having to sleep with me). It was impossible to get rid of it, even when we opened the door—and let in gusts of freezing wind.

I was forever battling the smoke. Maybe I was so muddled by it that I couldn't understand that Mother was not just sick, she was not just suffering from shortness of breath and bedsores. Mother was passing away.

My place was always down by the stove, crouching. It was my brother, like a most compassionate nurse, who was forever by Mother's side, giving her injections, lifting her. With my help, he would wash the bedsores that had formed and were beginning to fester on her thin body from rubbing against the straw mattress. We looked in vain for medication that might help. By some miracle, my brother managed to get a doctor to see her—a Jewish woman who had been evacuated from Leningrad. Like her fellow Leningrad evacuees, she enjoyed certain privileges. A Volga-German doctor, a political deportee like us, came once but he did not come back. Maybe he knew that it was hopeless, but maybe there were other reasons too. Yet the woman doctor came and continued coming often, even though she knew that she would not be paid and, in fact, that her coming could have potentially negative repercussions for her. She decided to give Mother the injections that had been sent to us by a doctor in Lviv the previous winter. These had to be administered intravenously and no other doctor here was willing to do it. The shots helped somewhat, even though medications for her cough and for her bedsores were still unavailable.

My brother was always out searching of food. Sometimes I went out too—whenever Hanusia could drag me away from the stove. Sometimes some of the other deportees would come and bring food for Mother, quite possibly giving away some meager supplies that they had received from Lviv. I would have loved to get at least a spoonful of sugar for her! Nevertheless she was eating less and less. She could not sleep, neither at night nor during the day. She was suffocating, and it was all due to the smoke. So I thought.

After one especially difficult night, my brother went out to fetch the doctor. I was squatting beside the stove, as always. Mother heaved a profoundly deep sigh.

"Mother, what is it? Mother, say something! You're choking! Should I give you an injection? Which one?"

I pulled out the syringe. But I didn't know the first thing about giving injections. I didn't know what to do. I ran out into the street. The sun was blindingly bright and the cold was freezing. It was noon. I wanted someone to come help me. But there was no one around. I went back in. How could I leave Mother alone when she was so sick? What was I supposed to do? My brother would have known—I only knew about the smoke.

"Mother, wait! He's coming back soon. Wait for him!"

Mother heaved another deep and heavy sigh.

By the time my brother returned, Mother lay still, with a smile on her face. Nothing was hurting her now. She seemed to have shrunk deep into her straw pallet; she was so tiny. And the smoke no longer choked her.

Now we would no longer be searching for food for Mother. Instead, we were looking for lumber to make a casket for her, a horse to transport it and a place to dig her grave. Our friends helped. When we were dressing her body we found that she had given all her clothes away to be bartered for food; only a very few things were left.

Mother lay on the table, smiling, and her body was cold, her hands white. Nevertheless, it was still Mother. I could rest my head against her shoulder hoping, waiting, that she would caress it.

We needed to cover her eyes with a small silk cloth—a *kytaika*—put her body into the coffin, seal it and carry it away on a sleigh over the snowy, frozen road—the very road by which we hoped Father would arrive from prison.

It was not I who walked behind the sleigh bearing the casket. That was someone else. I was still there with Mother.

131

This would be the late afternoon hour when she sometimes napped. Sometimes her pain would ease and then she would talk. Once, amazingly serene, she talked about the future. She wondered if, after Father returned to us, she would have the strength to survive the return trip home—as she had managed to survive the separation.

Another time she talked about her grandchildren, little Vlodko— and those still to be born—coming on Sundays to visit her. She talked about how she would cook their favorite foods and how she would play with them.

She said that if she had it to live all over again, she would have chosen the same path: beside Father and with Father, with all the same consequences, all the joys and all the tragedies.

Once, on a small piece of paper, she wrote down all our names—her special names for us when we were children—with all their diminutive forms. These were the last words written in her hand. Maybe this was her way of saying goodbye; maybe she knew.

Only I did not know; I was not fully conscious. I was confused, drugged by the smoke. And it was not I who walked behind the casket-bearing sleigh on that late afternoon. That was someone else.

*   *   *   *

The cemetery was located on the edge of the village, across from the hospital. Only one solitary tree grew there. My brother and our friends carried the coffin from the road to where the graves were and set it down on the snow-covered ground as they searched for the site that was to have been dug. Where is your grave, Mother?? It's gone!

Someone had stolen Mother's grave! Someone had come and buried someone else in the grave that had been prepared for Mother. After we asked around, we learned that it was someone from the hospital. We demanded that they dig another grave. However, it was already too late that day. It's not easy to dig a hole in this permafrost soil! The hole would have to be deep because of the wolves. Just for this night we had to lay her body into the stolen grave, to be shared with a stranger.

The next day at noon, the last day of the year, we walked to the cemetery together with a few of our deportee friends. A new gravesite had been prepared. It was located near the cemetery's solitary tree. Maybe that was how she wanted it. We dug up the coffin ourselves, lowered it into its new place and covered it with clumps of frozen earth.

Mother, forgive me for exposing your suffering, your wounds, your words—intended for us alone—and your final death sighs for the whole world to see.

I know that suffering and death is experienced personally and totally alone. As it is for you and so it is for us all! You always hated to expose your pain before others. Mother, forgive me, but how could I not speak? Do I dare remain silent?

Chapter 22 :

Amnesty

Looking out of my workplace window I could see the main road. It was the only entryway into the village for all cars, trucks and wagons, whether horse, oxen or camel-drawn. Everything brought in from the outside world and the rail depot had to cross the bridge and use this road.

Ever since amnesty for former Polish citizens had been declared, so many deportees were directing their gaze toward this road. It seemed that everyone had a relative—a father, a husband, a son or a daughter—imprisoned in a concentration camp. Now everyone was living with the hope—approaching a certainty—that they would be reunited soon.

No one talked about it, but every family anxiously made plans. They thought about finding room in their homes for their returning relatives to sleep. They thought about what they would serve them to eat. They wondered if the returnees would arrive by automobile or wagon. They limited their own food rations in order to save some for their dear family member who had suffered even greater deprivation. What would he look like? Oh, if the moment would just arrive! We all looked out of our windows and we waited.

*   *   *   *

A truck came to a stop outside our office. Behind the cab, I could see a grey head. For me every grey head was potentially my father's head. I wondered if I would recognize him.

What? Not recognize my own father?

The grey head lifted. It was some elderly gentleman—a stranger. He was someone else's father. He had trouble climbing over the truck's high bed rail. Slowly, with difficulty, leaning against a wheel, he lifted his legs. The bundle he was carrying made it awkward.

The driver stuck his head out the window—he saw the old man struggling to dismount and he encouraged him, "Come on, come on old man!" The words sounded harsh but there was no malice in his voice, only indifference. He was the driver for our agency.

"He could help him," I thought. I had to run out myself. My boss wasn't in the office, so I was out in a flash.

However the elderly gentleman had already climbed down. He stood there, gathering his belongings from the bundle that had fallen to the ground and come undone.

The driver started the truck and drove off, leaving me and the old man in a cloud of dust.

"Gosh, how thin and weak he looks," I thought to myself. I asked him who he was looking for. Which camp did he come from? Had he ever met my father?

His family came running. I had to turn away. I could not bear to see their reunion. This was a very private matter—their tears and their embraces, their silences and their words alternating.

As I walked back into the office, I saw another *lagernik*[17] standing there. They were so easily recognizable, even from afar. This one was not old but he was thin and bedraggled.

I asked him, "Who are you here to see?"

"Yes, I've heard the name, I know them," I told him. They lived in a kolhosp—but it was not nearby. Then he asked me about some other acquaintances. Their home, as it turned out, was down the next alley.

He walked ever so slowly, dragging his feet. He, too, carried a bundle in his hands. But he also had a teakettle—obviously a hard-won possession—his own tea kettle, what a remarkable treasure! He walked

---

17 *lagernik*=slang for inmate, usually a political prisoner of a Soviet prison labor camp; from the German word "Lager" (camp).

away and I didn't have a chance to ask him if he had ever seen my father. I wondered which prison camp he was being released from.

Enough! I had to get back to work!

At dusk, as I was going home, I could hear someone walking in the alley between the *rozvaliushky*. He heard my steps as well and he called to me to ask for directions. I could tell by his accent that he was a Pole. He had gotten lost amid the ruined homes. As I came up to him I could see that it was the man with the tea kettle. He had not been able to locate his family and he was going to spend the night with some friends, but he got lost.

The house where we lived was nearby, and although Mother was ill, it was summer, so we could make room for him somehow. There was room on top of the *peech*—the large tiled masonry oven. Now I could ask him which camp he had come from and if he had ever met Father.

He was an attorney and he knew Father from Lviv. They were never assigned to the same prison camp, but they had met once at a transfer station where they spent the night.

He told us what he knew. It was a good thing that it was night and too dark for him to see my face. I bit my knuckles to keep from crying out in pain. He told us how the prisoners fought for berths, and how Father was left out and how there was no place left for him to sleep. He told us that he remembered Father from Lviv as a defense attorney who, even when representing criminals, always believed in their capacity to reform. Remembering Father, I could not even imagine him becoming angry. Now I had to think about him surrounded by thugs, fighting for a place to sleep and a morsel of food.

The "gentleman with the tea kettle" spent the night on the ledge atop the masonry oven. He was so grateful that he was even ready to part with the teakettle. He said that my voice amid the dark and ruined houses was, for him, the "hand of God."

In the morning, he left to search for his family. I wondered if Father might be wandering around some strange alleyways, with a bundle in his hand and without a place to spend the night.

A few weeks later, another former inmate came to our house. He had learned that we lived here and he searched us out because he had been in the same prison camp as my father. This was another lawyer—a

Ukrainian. He was younger and healthier. He worked in a textile mill. He told us that Father had been declared an invalid and therefore his food rations were smaller.

I asked, "So, is he going hungry, then?"

There was no response to that question. Father had written to us not to waste our own resources on him. Maybe, he wrote, we could send him some onions or anything else that we did not need.

Father's former fellow inmate reassured us: "They aren't releasing everyone at the same time—one day they let out one group and the next another. His turn will come soon, maybe in a week or two."

We waited. Our eyes followed each truck that pulled into the village. Each grey head could be my father's.

Weeks passed. Months passed.

Then it was only the two of us. Mother was already resting under the solitary tree outside the village.

The elderly gentleman, whose family I saw meeting him outside my work place did not survive freedom. Like so many others, after his release from prison camp he contracted dysentery and died. True, he died surrounded by family who shut his eyes and gave him a proper burial—in a coffin in the village cemetery.

The "gentleman with the tea kettle" was left alone. We saw him occasionally walking around the village with his bundle, but now without the kettle. His family had already prepared documents to leave the area for some place where a military unit was being formed for General Anders' Polish army. They went to the southern provinces of Kazakhstan; from there they left for parts unknown. He himself did not have the necessary papers and his family did not want to take a chance trying to obtain them and then being forced to wait. Maybe eventually he also emigrated. I do not know.

The encouraging words from Father's comrade were not fulfilled. The procurator said, "It is true, amnesty has been declared, but we will not release him." People like Father were not being released.

We learned that he died one wintry day, at noon, in the camp infirmary. He starved to death. They released his jacket to us and in his pocket, we found a single garlic clove and a piece of string. Maybe it was something he used to tie his shoe.

A Cossack from Kuban, who had been in Father's camp barrack told us later that Father was never permitted to write anything; even the smallest piece of paper was taken away from him.

They threw his body into a common grave at night, with a note tied to his foot. Bribed with a bottle of vodka, the guards promised to mark the site. In the morning there was a small branch stuck into the frozen ground. This was the place!

Now the common grave is paved over; it's a street in some new town. And maybe somebody else's grey-haired father now strolls the street with his grandson. Perhaps he even knows that the town was built on human bones—the bones of imprisoned people who were never released, even though amnesty had been declared.

Chapter 23:

Prayers for the Repose of the Soul

At first, the sun-warmed wave of air that hit me as I walked out of my workplace seemed very pleasant. These were the first hot days of spring, but the office building with its thick walls of *saman* and its clay floors still hadn't released the damp cold trapped within. The sun had not yet had enough time to penetrate the walls and the ground to remove all signs of winter. Nevertheless, after taking just a few steps into the bright sun the palpable heat enveloped me like a densely woven cloth. Even before I reached the market place, the warmth, so pleasant at first, became a broiling mass, a transparent but viscose gel that filled all space and I had to make my way through it.

On the horizon, the hot air—visible between the widely scattered houses—shimmered and formed odd shapes. Indeed, mirages were possibly forming somewhere.

The road was deserted. Everyone was either out in the fields or else somewhere at work. It seemed that I was the only living creature still moving beneath this high sun and in its earth-scorching heat.

For a few moments, I took shelter under the shade of the trees that were planted and cultivated with such difficulty. But although I slowed my pace I could not rest in their comforting shade for long, I had to walk farther – out into the hot road.

I turned onto a side path that connected one road with another. It bordered on an open expanse that was neither steppe nor cultivated land. Only the fortunate few had their own well to water the soil and actually grow a garden. Mostly, only grass and wormwood grew here. Before long, the wormwood would grow to a height of a human and soon a forest of the bitter-scented grayish-green shrubs would be growing along this path. Now the parched earth rose beneath my feet leaving a trail of dust clouds behind me.

Far off I saw someone approaching me. Another living being in this broiling barren wasteland! As he drew nearer, I recognize him. He was once the estate administrator for the composer Tchaikovsky's sister. He was an ethnic Russian, but he had lived in Ukraine for so many years that it became very dear to him. When he was exiled to Kazakhstan he brought with him, among his most treasured possessions, a man's embroidered tunic and a wide brimmed peasant straw hat, both typical of the style worn in the village where the estate was located. He said that he was saving the tunic for his burial. The hat he wore to preserve his graying head from the broiling sun that flowed down like molten lava. He could barely walk, his swollen aged feet—like dead wood—painfully shuffling, one tiny step at a time. In his hand he held a small canister. He was probably headed for the dairy to get some whey. Sometimes it was made available. Not only could it slake one's hunger and thirst, it was also said to have medicinal properties for those with heart ailments.

I would see him sometimes standing in line at the dairy. Even though his clothing was patched and shabby, and his aged body bent, he nevertheless retained a certain dignity. I always wondered, "Why? What offense did he commit to be deported to this place?" It was possible to pose that question too many times, and too many times it would be useless to await an answer.

We passed, greeting each other. And then, once more, I was alone on this scorching open expanse. Off to the side I saw the wooden wall of the market—made up of backs of single stalls placed side by side. I was amazed that no one had pulled the boards apart yet and stolen them for firewood during the winter. Here and there, there were holes, but all-in-all the tables and benches were more or less intact. Of course, there was a night watchman guarding it.

I had no real reason to walk through the marketplace, but as long as I was in the vicinity, I thought I would. Maybe someone had some food to sell or to barter.

I passed the battered wooden wall surrounding the market place and entered the square, hot as a frying pan. Only two old grannies were seated on a bench by the wall. Sacks of sunflower seeds and coarsely chopped homegrown tobacco were displayed for sale on the table in front of them. Next to the sacks stood glasses filled almost to overflowing with the seeds and the tobacco. The glasses were the measure by which they were sold—a ruble apiece. The old women seemed to stir as they heard someone approaching, but when they saw that it was only me, they lowered their heads once more and returned to their napping. A dog, rolled up into a ball, was sleeping under the bench; he too lifted his head and then replaced it on top of his paws.

From the opposite end of the broiling square another figure approached. The disheveled grey hair and beard hid a face. Beneath the thick eyebrows that somehow had remained black, shiny narrow slits of eyes glared out onto the world. They slowly scanned the area before skittering off to one side. The big-framed old man was tall, skinny and bent, clad in rags and—as usual—he carried a broom and a bucket in his hands. He had a swinging gait—it looked as though he was shifting weight from one foot to the other. As he walked, he mumbled to himself. Whenever I met him I tried to make out what it was that he was mumbling—but I never could. Sometimes it seemed that he was praying and sometimes the bristly knots of his beard simply seemed to absorb muffled curses.

It was said that he was once a priest—perhaps of some lower order. Now after many years in prison, he had been exiled to this place. The only job he was allowed to have was to clean the village office buildings; hence the broom and bucket. Whenever he passed one of us he would raise his normally lowered eyes and shoot us an electrifying glance, but then, just as quickly, his eyes would return to hide under his eyelashes or shift off to the sides.

The locals made fun of him; they thought he was insane. Maybe, indeed, after surviving the prisons he was mentally unbalanced or maybe.... It sometimes seemed to me that this image of a lame-brained old man who talked to himself while cleaning the village toilets, was a defensive mask, a protective armor that shielded this tortured and maltreated old priest.

Once, in passing him on the road, when there were no other people around, I greeted him in God's name.[18] He looked startled and his dark eyes took on a sharp, suddenly fully alert look, but then he picked up his pace and hurried off. From then on he would observe me carefully. He was probably wondering if my greeting was a provocation or a sincere praise of God.

Now, all alone, he approached me on this dusty market square… The grannies with their sunflower seeds and their tobacco had sunk into a deep sleep—it was as if they had ceased to exist.

I made a sudden on-the-spot decision. I stepped in front of him so that he had to stop. I looked directly into his gray-bearded face and quickly asked: "Would you be willing to do a *panakhyda*[19] service for my mother?"

We had buried my mother in unconsecrated ground and in a casket made of wood procured with great difficulty. Once a Polish priest—at the time Anders' military units were being organized—came to the village and blessed all the graves. And now I was asking this man to say a *panakhyda*.

The old man looked at me fearfully, and then he looked to each side, and finally behind. There was no one around. He mumbled something—not to me, but to himself and into his beard. He squirmed, as if he wanted to run away, but I was an obstacle in his path. I could see that he did not trust me and that he was afraid. Therefore I said, "Don't be afraid. I am a deportee, like you. Tell me, will you do it? Just tell me where and when."

We heard voices; someone was approaching. The old man swept past me, swinging his arms with their attached broom and pail, like an animal who suddenly found a way out of a trap. He left me behind in a cloud of the broiling marketplace dust.

That evening I was walking down the broad street that led into the village where Mother's grave was located. Behind me, the sun was setting, surrounded by puffy clouds edged with gold. As I came near the first

---

18 A commonly accepted greeting among believers in pre-Soviet Ukraine was *Slava Isusu Khrystu* ("Glory to Jesus Christ")

19 A panakhyda is an Eastern Christian (both Orthodox and Catholic) memorial service for the dead.

Kazakh houses of the village, I ran into him again. The blazing sun had turned his disheveled hair into a bright red halo. He seemed to recognize me and slowed his gait so that we would meet. He looked furtively to the left and right and over his shoulder and then he stopped. He spoke quickly, sputtering, "Come tomorrow. In the evening. That house over there." He pointed with the broom he carried. "Knock. Say you have come to see Mikhail. Bring some bread—for the *panakhyda*."

Then he turned off to the side, quickly disappearing among the houses.

I still had a little flour left—but no fuel. My neighbor baked a small loaf for me.

Evening came. Once more, the sun painted the dust that rose beneath my feet in clouds of gold and red tones. I made my way among the long, low and narrow Kazakh houses until I found the one I needed.

I knocked on the door. Silence. I felt, rather than saw or heard, an eye, pressed to the crack in the door, scrutinizing me carefully. After a long minute, I heard a raspy voice whisper, "Why are you here? Whom do you want to see?"

"I'm here to see Mikhail."

Another long minute of silent debate, followed by a sound of something being moved, something that held the door in place. The door opened. I walked into a pitch-black maw of a room and stood in the darkness for another minute. To one side I could make out two specks of light—probably cracks in the door to the main room of the house. Whoever it was who opened the door for me melted into the gloomy darkness that surrounded me. Gradually, after a minute or two as my eyes became accustomed to the dark, I could make out the entryway that also served as a stable, which was typical of a Kazakh house. Away from the stable and to the right there was an even deeper darkness, probably a hallway; facing me directly was a door with the two bright cracks of light. I went up to it and knocked again. Without asking any questions, someone cracked the door very, very slowly and peered at me.

"Who are you here to see?"

"I'm here for Mikhail."

The door opened a little wider. The tiny room with its dirt floor and little window had only one piece of furniture, a narrow bed covered with a patched blanket. A large masonry oven-stove divided the room in half. The person who let me in was an old Chinese man dressed in a grey cotton suit.

"Come in," he said and he led me past the stove to the other half of the room which was just like the first. Whoever lived there was not in now. There was a small door here too. The Chinese man knocked quickly and repeatedly.

"Mikhail, someone is here to see you."

On the other side of the door, I could hear a woman's voice—but I couldn't quite make out what she was saying. Then, standing in the doorway I saw the *staretz*-Mikhail.[20] It was the first time I had ever seen him without his broom and pail.

Silently, he indicated that I should enter. To the Chinese fellow he said, "Keep guard, Zhan-Enden."

This room was identical to the previous two. In the corner, there was a stove—the kind they call a "Russian stove." Seated on a stool in front of it was an old woman, her gaze fixed. I quickly realized that she was blind. When I entered, she fell silent. But as soon as the door closed, the steady stream of angry words resumed. It was her voice that I heard through the door earlier. Now I could make out what she was saying even though in her anger she swallowed half the syllables and slurred the words together.

"There you go again. Why are you looking for trouble? Haven't you had enough already? Why are you letting people in?"

As she ranted, Mikhail spoke to her in an even, soothing voice.

"There, there now, Auntie. We have to do this. Her mother died, and she is asking for a *panakhyda* for the repose of her soul."

"Auntie" continued to grumble, although in a slightly less agitated voice. She went on and on even as the old man, unexpectedly agile, crawled up on top of the stove so that only the soles of his worn shoes were visible. He reached down behind the stove somewhere and pulled out a thick book and a bundle of some kind. He untied the bundle and put on an *epitrachyl*.[21] In less than a minute, the old man had disappeared, and in his place a grey-haired, grey-bearded priest appeared.

---

20 *Staretz*= literally "old man." Used colloquially, a term for a spiritual man, not necessarily a priest, recognized for his piety.

21 *Epitrachyl*= Ecclesial vestment; the Byzantine equivalent of the Latin *stole*

The priest began to sing the prayers of the *panakhyda* in an aged, slightly raspy voice.

The angry Auntie grew silent. After a minute her voice returned—to make the appropriate responses to the priest's prayers.

I stood against the wall of this small room and listened to the prayers – not those exactly of my own faith, but still directed to the same God. Every now and then, the old priest seemed to forget himself and allowed his voice to grow in strength, but then Auntie would wave her hand and, in between verses, she would say, "Softer, softer, for heaven's sake! They'll hear you." So, like a wave, the chanting would become more subdued again, borne serenely along on a semi-audible stream.

I closed my eyes and reminded myself that this was still me—the same person who, not too long ago, had walked the streets of Lviv, with my mother waiting for me at home. Here I was now, in this tiny room of a Kazakh house, listening to the chanting of a clandestine *panakhyda* for the repose of her soul. Of course, she was no longer with us. But she would have found it so interesting to hear me tell her about the priest who hid his prayer books and vestments in a secret hiding place behind the stove. Even more interesting was the way he hid himself behind the mask of a half-witted, doddering old man with a tangled beard.

For a moment, I lost touch with reality. Everything seemed surreal and improbable. I was sure that everything would disappear and I could go home to Mother.

The chanting stopped abruptly and that brought me back to reality. The old man fell silent and listened anxiously. There was some activity in the neighboring room. Soon a reassuring voice called from behind the door, "It's just me, Mikhail; everything is alright." The chanting continued smoothly. After the prayers were finished, auntie was completely calm; she asked about Mother, when and how she had died. Then she added, "I will pray for her."

The priest did not say anything more. Silently he crawled back behind the stove to hide his prayer book and the bundle with the *epitrachyl*. He was still silent as I said my goodbyes and left.

In the neighboring room, the one that previously had been empty I saw our acquaintance, Tchaikovsky's sister's administrator. He nodded to me, conspiratorially. Perhaps it was he who convinced Mikhail to trust me.

I walked out onto the street, dark now that the sun had already set. From where I stood, I could see the lonely tree that grew over my mother's grave. No one at home awaited me, no one with whom I could share the story of this strange old man. But I suppose Mother knew everything by now anyway and maybe she was gazing down at me from the heights of this starry sky with its foreign and unfamiliar constellations.

Looking back, I saw a figure standing in the doorway. Was it the old man who walked the streets of the village, broom and pail in hand, mumbling incoherently into his beard or was it the priest who sang the prayers of the secret *panakhyda* and hid his prayer book and vestments behind the stove?

Now, once more, I felt that I was the only living being on the face of the earth, slowly making my way over this wide expanse. The pale strip of the road lay beneath me and the high dome of an inky sky, marked with traces of a violet and crimson setting sun on the horizon, hung above. The houses had turned into darkened mounds and behind me, the dark silhouette of the solitary tree swayed over my mother's grave.

Chapter 29

Mirror, Mirror on the Wall

I entered the waiting room to the administrative director's office with a slip of paper in my hand. It read, "Issue to the bearer one pair of women's *valianky*." But the clerk at the storehouse refused. There was only one pair left and he had to keep them there.

"Somebody might need them in the future—*somebody*. Do you understand?"

This time I refused to give in. The director of the factory, Pavel Pavlovich himself, had given me this voucher and he promised that if I went to the central office I would get my *valianky*. The soles of the oversize men's shoes, with their bent-back toes, that I had been wearing, had split away across the middle. I tried tying them together with a string, but it was impossible to walk in them. My feet were always wet—and here it was, only autumn. What would happen come winter? As head accountant, after all, I had to get to work. See, I brought with me the financial statement for the past three quarters.

The storehouse manager shrugged his shoulders, thought about it for a while and then sent me to the director—the Head Administrative Director.

I sank into the deep chair, pushed my *shapka-ushanka*[22] back from my forehead and waited. The waiting room was cold; it was hardly

---

22 *shapka-ushanka*= cap with earflaps

warmer than the street outside. A secretary entered and quickly flitted across the room and then just as quickly flitted back again. She was dressed—as were all administrative office employees— in a beret, worn atilt, and a quilted jacket. Once she asked me why I had come and then she told me to wait. So I waited. She kept walking back and forth from the director's office, always with papers in her hand. She paid no attention to me.

I was getting really sleepy because I had traveled all night to get there. To keep awake I needed to move around. I rose and began pacing, a few steps in one direction, and a few in the other. Suddenly—who was that? There was someone facing me. I stopped for a moment, but then looking up, I quickly turned away and froze in place. It was a full-length mirror and I saw myself reflected in it. I stood rooted there, with my back turned away. I did not want to look at myself. Better to sit down, or something—anything—as long as it was away from that mirror.

I couldn't even remember when I had last looked into a mirror. Maybe it was when Mother was still well and Father, although far away, was still alive. I was not alone then. I had a tiny compact mirror—a gift from that special someone. I always carried it with me in my pocket like an amulet. I would sometimes pull it out to look at myself and comb my hair.

Mother didn't like it if I became careless about my appearance. Now Mother was gone. Oh Mother! Everyone was gone! Beyond that cold fact nothing else mattered.

Still I thought, maybe I should take a peek in the mirror? But why? I really didn't care! Only one thing mattered—I had to get my *valianky*, because otherwise I knew I would freeze to death.

But I could not sit still. The very awareness that there was a mirror in the room was too much for me. It was like another presence in the room. I rose ever so slowly. With my eyes downcast, almost stealthily, I approached the mirror.

I would look up when I got there.

Now! Now I would look!

Suddenly the secretary flitted in. I froze as if caught in some criminal act. But she wasn't paying attention to me. A moment later, and she flitted out. I was alone again. Alone with the mirror.

"Enough of this silliness! Making such a big deal out of looking at yourself in a mirror!"

Two more energetic steps toward the mirror. Eyes downcast.

I began by looking at my reflected feet. There they were, the familiar old shoes, tied together with string to keep the soles from coming apart. In the mirror, they looked even larger, with their upturned scuffed noses and the string, tied in bows falling off to the side.

Just above the shoes were two skinny legs wrapped in heavy grey socks. They had been sent to us from Lviv when packages were still allowed. Then the hem of the long coat, almost touching my ankles. It had been Father's old coat.

My eyes traveled quickly upward, taking measure of myself. The sides of the oversize coat were tightly wrapped one over one another and tied with a belt at the waist to make for greater warmth.

Finally, my eyes rose to my face.

"That's me," I whispered, "that's me!"

I took a hand out of its huge mitten and lifted it up to my face. The person in the mirror also raised her hand. It was reddish-blue in color, swollen and covered with frostbite lesions. It touched the face where a red patch of frostbite from the previous year looked like greasepaint applied by a clown.

The hand dropped.

Now I couldn't tear my eyes away from the woman in the mirror. It seemed to be me, but maybe it was someone else? The small triangular face looked even smaller under the wing-like flaps of the *shapka*. Peering out beneath the cap were eyes.

They appeared to be mine—but somehow they were different. How were they different? The eyes in the mirror were tense, both amazed and wary; they seemed to be searching, waiting for something.

They were old.

Again, I touched my face to make sure that it really was me. I turned my head first to one side and then to the other. I adjusted the *shapka*, pushed it off my forehead and then down again. I measured myself from head to toe.

Now I really was afraid that the secretary would come in and interrupt my reflections. I wanted to know what had happened to me. What was I like? Would the mirror help?

Those tightly compressed lips. That unfamiliar frown—it belonged to a stranger.

For a minute, I closed my eyes and tried to remember my former self—what did I look like? I did not know. It was all so different now. Not only the shrunken face with its frostbitten blotch, not only this huge coat, wrapped tightly around me and tied—like a sheaf—with a belt, not only these oversized men's shoes. Something else had changed. It was the eyes. These eyes held no expectations, they held no hope; they had stopped caring.

What would Mother say? She would be horrified. She wouldn't recognize me. She hated it whenever I became apathetic. And "he"? He, too, would never recognize me. Forget him! There was no "him." He would never see me again.

Never again. Those words reverberated as if I heard them now for the first time. Something moved in the depth of my soul. Mother hated the words "Never" and "Apathy." She forbade them.

But I didn't care. It was all the same to me.

Or was it?

They liked it when I laughed. I grimaced into the mirror. It was supposed to be a smile! Rays of wrinkles around the eyes, teeth showing between cracked lips, the frostbitten splotch rising up near the eyes. But the eyes did not change, they didn't smile. They didn't care.

I brought my face close to the mirror.

"Is that you? Who are you?" I murmured.

The door creaked open.

"You! The director will see you now."

It all disappeared. Only the *valianky* were still important. Where was that note? What was I going to say? I had it all prepared—and now I've forgotten it all. Wait! How was I going to begin?

"What is it you want? Don't waste time."

"*Valianky*... here's the note... *valianky*. The storehouse clerk didn't want to give them to me." I was not making any sense. I pointed at my shoes.

The director stared for a moment. He read the note.

"Oh, *valianky*. That's right, you're the head bookkeeper. But why did you come here? To get your *valianky*? Oh no, I see you have the account balances. Good. You'll get the boots."

Leaving the store with my new *valianky* I thought, "My feet will be warm. I didn't come this far for nothing. They will last for two winters. Two winters. God! Two more—and then how many?"

But there was something more than just contentment with the *valianky*. I sensed something else. There was a crack in my wooden apathy. Something had happened to me. What? Some thoughts, some memories. Why?

Then I knew… it was the mirror.

Chapter 25:
Love Has More Than One Name

The place was called Br-Tobie, "Lone Mountain," and it leapt out of the steppe unexpectedly, as if the earth itself had hurled it from its innermost recesses.

Long, grey houses climbed up the slope of the mountain. They were hardly visible, blending in as they did with the grey steppe. Mounds of manure, still partly covered by a grimy snow, stood steaming in front of each house. The houses were arranged in such a way as to form three sides of a rectangle. The fourth side was open to the steppe and into this opening a train of ox-drawn wagons had entered and was waiting to take us away somewhere, out into this steppe, past the Lone Mountain, past Br-Tobie.

A stiff wind was blowing. It carried sand and pebbles and last year's stubble of grass which stung our faces and eyes. Aside from clumps of dead grass there was not a blade or bush to be seen anywhere.

"This looks like the gateway to Dante's inferno," I thought.

The inhabitants of this outpost came out of their houses, high-cheek-boned Kazakhs, men in their pointy fur-lined caps, women in dirty and tattered veils. Also among them, it turned out, were some deportees, like us. They had been brought here yesterday—and now here they were in this state cattle farm. They had no idea what they were going to be doing or how they were going to survive. We exchanged impressions and unanswerable questions.

This was accompanied by gusts of wind that drove thick clouds. Again and again—either the cloud's dark shadows chilled us to the bone, or the hot sun's rays burned us.

Our encounters here were brief. The ox-drawn convoy was leaving. In all the confusion, I found my attention drawn to the image of a petite young woman which was seared into my memory. She had kept apart from our conversations and questions. Standing in the doorway of her house, her hands convulsively twisting, her wide hazel eyes staring ahead, she looked helpless, almost child-like, as she seemed to search for something in the vast steppe before her. Her pale face was framed by fair hair and it made her eyes look large and dark. Her clothes—the high-heeled shoes and the city-styled coat—were strangely out of place here. Everything about her seemed totally unrelated to this environment.

Once we were on the road again, someone told me that they had known her back in Lviv. She was a specialist of some sort at the Ossolineum Institute but she also had a reputation of being a spoiled, affected girl who liked to spend her free time in cafes and dance clubs. She was always surrounded by young men. They all tried to overcome her caprices and break through to her heart, the heart of a beautiful and fascinating young woman. Still, it seemed that no man was ever good enough for her. Maria toyed with men—first with one, then another—but none was ever able to hold her attention for long.

This story, told by my fellow travelers, fixed in my memory the image of the dark eyed young woman with her fine-featured face and her halo of blonde hair. Perhaps, if it were not for this information, she might have faded from my memory along with many other impressions of that ox-drawn journey through the melancholy steppe with its hellishly howling wind.

That bitter first winter finally passed. Its vise-like freezing cold, starvation, and disease crushed not only the deportees, but even the local population. Then a second winter passed. Now we were living in a settlement with a few more trees and water. I had a slightly better job. One day when I was on my lunch break, I saw a woman walking out of the *kolhosp* office building. Wrapping a shawl around her, she walked along the path that led past my window. There was something familiar about her. The way she carried herself, her gait and her movements all indicated, even from afar, that this was not a local woman. Walking behind her was a tall, trim man. As they drew near, I recognized her; it was Maria. Yes, she had changed somewhat, but there was still that same elegance about her now-shawl-clad figure. When the man came closer into view, I had to catch my breath. Half of his face was one enormous scar. It was as if someone had cut away part of his face and then sewn the rest of it back together in bumpy strips.

I had several opportunities to talk with him later. I could see that his jaw had been broken, making his speech barely intelligible. It was hard to look at him directly in the face. Sometimes it is possible to grow accustomed to seeing some disfigurement, but looking at him, it was impossible to ignore.

His name was Tymish. He was a Siberian native. His parents, or maybe his grandparents, had come here during the Tsarist rule. As a young man, he had been sent to the big city to study. It was there that he suffered his tragedy. There were several versions of what had happened. The most believable story had him falling in love with a girl who then left him. He shot himself in the head. His life was saved, but his face was grotesquely scarred and his speech permanently impaired.

Our first winter, unusually severe even by local standards with its amounts of snow and its horrific blizzards, was even harsher in the settlement where Maria lived with her sister. There, among the primitive Kazakhs, far away from other outposts, they would have faced certain death if Tymish had not arrived because of some kolhosp business and helped them. Because of his care and efforts, they were able to survive and later move to our village. He was so extraordinarily kind and gentle that Maria decided to link her fate to his. It is not for me to know her motivation. Maybe it was gratitude, maybe despair, maybe pity for his disfigurement, or maybe it was something else. Love is never single-faceted. Feminine caprice—especially in such an exaltedly beautiful woman like Maria—might have been reason enough.

And so we would see them every morning as they went to work and every evening when they returned. She, walking in her measured, graceful gait, wrapped in her shawl, deftly avoiding all the uneven ruts in the path. He—taking long masculine strides—walked behind her or arm-in-arm beside her, wherever the path was wide enough.

That was the second picture that I have of Maria in my mind: the two of them walking side-by-side, with Tymish bending over her in a sensitive, protective way. From a distance, they would appear to be just an ordinary couple. But if you came near, close enough to see his disfigured face, you would know that these two had been united by some strange twist of fate.

Time went on. The war ended. Amnesty was declared. The deported population began to talk about that which until now had existed only in our thoughts and dreams—returning home. Hope energized everyone; somehow now, the surrounding sun-baked steppe, the grey houses and the harsh winds did not seem quite as dread-inspiring. There was hope now that it could all be left behind, like a bad dream.

People applying for repatriation were being registered. More and more, we were talking about where we would live, what we would do, whom we would meet back home. All in all a lively excitement was felt among the deportees. We all couldn't wait for departure.

Finally, everyone was being assembled in Br-Tobie, awaiting transport. The wait was long, lasting several weeks, which led many to moments of doubt. What if we wouldn't be allowed to leave after all? In the end, our hope was vindicated. Here was Maria's sister among the returnees. But where was Maria? She was not going to leave.

She came to see her sister off; to say goodbye. Maria had decided that she could not leave with Tymish. What kind of future could he possibly have back home —not knowing the language or the customs, not having a profession? She didn't say anything about his disfigurement. People here had become accustomed to it, but there—it could easily become an additional impediment.

Tymish tried to persuade her, "Go! Maybe I will follow later." Nevertheless, she refused to emigrate. She refused to go alone. He had suffered one tragedy already. Someone had abandoned him once before—someone he had trusted. Maybe, she said, someday, they could go together.

I saw Maria for the last time as our train slowly left the station. We crowded the wide-open door of the boxcar that was taking us away. There she was, her small figure wrapped in a shawl in the middle of the dreary and empty station, silhouetted against the background of the treeless Br-Tobie. It seemed to me that I could hear her trembling.

Tymish, with his tall figure and his terrible face, stood next to Maria as she gently leaned back on his shoulder. The train crept along ever so slowly. She could still hop on; there was still one last chance!

We were all silent, unable to say a word. What could we possibly say? Maria's sister stood next to me. I hugged her and felt her trembling, as if in a fever, holding back tears.

Slowly the train passed the spot where Maria was standing: motionless, firm, seemingly petrified. Just one single movement, it seemed, and her determination would break. Slowly we passed her. We leaned out of the boxcar opening as long as possible. The two figures continued standing there, immutable, in the same spot, slowly vanishing in the distance.

A strong wind whipped up and started blowing sand and pebbles. The figures disappeared and, behind them, the Lone Mountain—Br Tobie disappeared too.

Chapter 26:
The Easter Egg

For several weeks now my brother had been lying in the Semipalatynsk Typhus Hospital. He was taken there directly from the train that was bringing him from Krasnoyarsk after amnesty had been declared. While still on the train he felt the onset of fever and then there was no denying it—this was typhus.

He had managed to buy an upper berth for thirty rubles. As he lay there in a fever, he worried that someone would guess that he was ill with typhus. He knew that then he would be taken off the train, and be put away in some Siberian hole of a backwater hospital, where no one would ever learn of his whereabouts. So he waited until the train reached Semipalatynsk before he asked his fellow travelers to notify the authorities that he was sick.

They removed him from the train, took him to the hospital and detached his rail car to disinfect it. Before he lost consciousness he wrote to me, telling me what had happened. It was evident from his writing that he was beginning to slip into unconsciousness; the last few lines of the letter were incoherent.

With some difficulty I found out where he was hospitalized. Then, every day, together with a group of other people—Kazakhs, Russians, Azeris, Jews and Poles—I would stand for hours outside the one-story building that served as a hospital. I bartered personal items to buy milk, the only food that was still available, and had the nurse take it to him.

Since I had given her a little gift, I was able to prevail upon her to let me come into the hospital corridor where, as if by chance, she would leave the door open to the ward where he lay. I could see his shaved head resting on the hospital pillow. After some time, when he regained consciousness, he would turn his head in my direction and smile weakly. However, later, when he developed pleurisy, a result and complication of the typhus, he lost consciousness again and I could no longer see him smile.

The nurse advised me to take his watch and wedding band—hinting that otherwise they might be stolen. I worried, however, that if I took them it would feed into his feverish paranoia. The notes that he had the nurse pass to me, at times, appeared to be written in a delirium. He wrote repeatedly that he was being stalked and persecuted.

The hospital gates often remained closed to visitors. At that time, packages for patients were not being accepted nor was information regarding a patient's condition given out. The crowd at the gate had no choice but just to stand there and wait. Any hospital employee that appeared would be mobbed with requests and shouts in many different languages, as everyone tried to learn some news about "their" patient. It was always in vain.

We waited in the bitter cold, huddling together for warmth. From time to time the gate would open and a straw-covered sleigh would appear. Beneath the straw, the bare feet of the most recently deceased patient were visible. People in the crowd would moan and weep. No one knew who had died. We started looking in through the hospital windows into the wards, attempting to recognize our people. In an attempt to find "our" patients we started looking through the hospital windows into the wards. We pressed our faces to the windowpanes. The shaved heads lying on their pillows all looked identical. I felt a sudden sense of relief when I recognized, on the little table next to his bed, the bottle filled with milk that I brought yesterday. As I peered more closely, I saw his wristwatch on his hand. He was still alive!

Easter was coming. My brother was improving. More and more, I saw how he would lift his head and smile in my direction or even give me a little wave of the hand. I decided that somehow we had to celebrate Easter together.

Friends had managed to get some flour and bake a not-very-white but still tasty, Ukrainian Easter bread—a *babka*. I boiled and dyed an egg in onionskins; then I cut it in half. Together with a sprig of greenery, I wanted these to be delivered to him. Standing by the window, I would eat the other half of the egg—and so we would share our Easter egg.[23]

I went to the nurse and asked her to give him my special foods, now wrapped in a clean handkerchief. She opened the little package to check if there was anything in it that would be inappropriate for a patient recovering from typhus. Her eyes fell on the dyed egg-half.

"What's this? Half of an egg? A dyed egg-half?"

The nurse was young, but perhaps she still remembered something from when celebrating Easter was still allowed. At first, her face registered surprise—and then apprehensiveness. No, she would not allow this—she might be accused of taking part in a religious ritual.

Suddenly this egg-half, unblessed, and dyed in onionskins, took on an unexpectedly weighty significance that I sensed I needed to communicate to her. No one was nearby, so I explained that according to an old tradition, by dividing and sharing an egg we wish blessings upon one another, blessings so powerful, that they come true. I had an extra egg—also dyed—and I reached out to give it to her.

"Please," I said, "Take it and may your wishes be fulfilled."

The nurse looked around carefully and then quickly hid the egg in her pocket. Rewrapping my package into its handkerchief, she nodded to me and walked away. When she reached the doorway she turned and said, "Go stand by the window. I will tell him that you are going to be there. I will give him the egg and your good wishes."

A minute later I was standing by the window. I saw the nurse bending over him. It was evident that she was explaining something. She helped him to sit up. He turned his head toward the window and, smiling, raised his egg-half to his lips—while outside the window, I ate mine. Meanwhile the nurse pretended to be straightening his bed linens, secretly shielding him from other patients' view. She then waved

---

23   At the beginning of the first meal after the liturgy on Easter morning, in keeping with the tradition of Eastern Christian Churches, it is customary among Ukrainian families to break the fast by sharing an egg divided among those present along with the Easter bread, both of which had been blessed.

to me and walked away. I came close to the window and whispered the ancient Easter greeting: "*Khrystos Voskres*!—Christ Is Risen!" I saw his lips moving in response, "*Vo Istynu Voskres*!—Truly He Is Risen!"

Chapter 27:
Going Home

The rail car shook, squeaked, moaned; sometimes it even seemed to jump around. We were most acutely aware of its erratic movements at night. During the day, the car seemed more peaceful, but maybe that was because then our attention was being directed elsewhere. There was always something going on, and people were always engaged in conversation. This was especially true during those first few days of bustling activity, as everyone tried to arrange their belongings so as to make a "bed" for themselves and their children in the best way possible. Once everything was done—as far as the limited space in this boxcar that was to be our home for the three-week journey allowed—the activity died down. Now the conversations centered not so much on the past but ran ahead into the future. It became obvious that everyone was thinking (and not without some trepidation) about future reunions with family and friends back home—as well as remembering those with whom they would never meet again. Conversations became less and less general. All those things that had united us gradually disappeared in proportion to the widening distance between Dzhangis Tob'ie and us.

Still, even during periods of daytime silence, the car's wide-open door, with only a crossbar for safety, continued to attract everyone's attention. Even while lying in an upper berth one could look out onto the countryside with its grayish steppe and its infrequent islands of flowers—either bright red or so intensely yellow that they appeared to be gold.

If I managed to force my way to the open door and, sitting down, let my legs dangle off the edge, I could see the ground fleeing beneath the train. It was like an enormously broad gray cloth that was being measured off in the same way that a shopkeeper uses a yardstick to measure off a bolt of fabric… one meter…then another. Here the steppe, with telephone poles as measures, passed before our eyes, on and on into infinity.

As I sat there, with my eyes closed, I was painfully reminded of my youthful trips on the narrow gauge train along the Limnytsia River to Pidliute and beyond—on and on all the way up to Char. Beneath my feet, I could see the ravines and the silvery, snake-like Limnytsia at the bottom, or the vertical mountain wall that came so close to the train that it made me want to pull in my legs to keep them from being crushed. Sometimes the grass tickled my bare feet, or sprinkled them with dew or recently fallen rain.

At night, maybe because the rail car was quiet and our attention was not being diverted, or maybe because the train was traveling faster then, the car groaned and banged noisily. Sometimes its cracking sounds grew so loud that it seemed the car would come apart at any moment. Every board in the walls of the car jumped, each in its own direction. In the quiet of the night, the popping sounds echoed loudly in the steppe. From time to time, the train would emit a groan and the railcar would shudder and leap even higher.

I put my hand up and touched the wall behind my head. Placing my palm where two boards came together, I really felt them moving in opposite directions. It heightened my anxiety. Maybe, then, this rail car could collapse like a house of cards, spilling all of us across the grey desert steppe.

The locomotive's whistle pierced the night. It made getting back to sleep completely impossible for me. I sat upright on the edge of my bunk and let my feet dangle. For a minute, I listened to make sure that my movements hadn't wakened anyone else. Carefully, I dropped first one foot then the other. I felt around for the berth beneath and slowly, quietly, let myself down.

The moon cast a bright rectangle of light – the open door—onto the center of the car floor. Deep shadows hid everything else. Holding on to the crossbeam I sat down on the edge of the car opening and let my feet dangle again. The car roared hollowly past the emptiness of some town and then rushed on, thundering and creaking rhythmically.

*   *   *   *

The adults sat on benches in the middle of the narrow-gauge platform bed, the so-called "lorry," and conversed. Every now and then, a mother's worried voice would reach us children as we sat with our feet dangling over the lorry's edge, "Watch out, or you'll fall off!"

*   *   *   *

Somehow, that annoyed me then. Oh, but now, how very much I would love to hear that worried-sounding, protective "Watch out!" But I won't.

All of these people were going back to their own families; they were always thinking of them. Even now, their thoughts, their dreams, ran on ahead of this train, and they envisioned reunions somewhere off in the distance.

Only two days ago, we were all reduced to a common denominator. Now, everyone was living with an anticipated future. These thoughts soothed and lulled them to sleep and kept them from hearing the night groans of the railcar.

I had nothing to think about. I was traveling into an empty void. Where to, exactly? I didn't even know. I was sure only of the place I was leaving behind... leaving it as far away as possible. I didn't know where I was going and I couldn't imagine that somewhere, someone might be waiting for me.

Whenever I visualized a reunion... any reunion... their reunions... I imagined melodramatic scenes like those in a silent film, where all emotion is conveyed in over-exaggerated facial expressions and broad dramatic gestures.

At night, the awareness of the unknown and the open nothingness before me was heightened and became almost tangible. I couldn't sleep, I couldn't dream of any future; so I listened to the boxcars groaning.

After some time sitting on the edge of the open door, I sensed that I was not alone. At first, I only sensed it, then after a while, peering into the shadows behind the door I saw that someone, swathed in a dark wrap, was leaning against the doorway. Before I could make out who it was, I heard her voice, "Be careful, don't fall asleep. Move back a little."

I knew this woman by sight. I remembered that her name was Zosia. She asked me the same question that everyone was asking: "Where are you going? Where will your people meet you?"

The question hurt. I didn't want to say, "Nowhere, no one will meet me." It seemed to me that if I spoke those words aloud they became an irrevocable certainty. I learned that if I didn't want to answer a question I could ask one in return.

"And you, Zosia, you are going to Lublin? That's just beyond the border. You'll be among the first to meet your family."

I said this because someone told me that she had received a letter from her husband, a professor, I think, at the University of Lublin. But there was no answer. Maybe she hadn't heard me.

"Besides your husband do you have other family there?"

I thought she would now begin talking. I imagined a gentleman with flowers … embraces …maybe tears… maybe her mother…maybe still someone else. But there was no answer. So I remained silent. I sensed that she wanted to talk. That's how it always was. I don't know why everyone always wanted to reveal their lives to me, the youngest person in this boxcar. I heard so many intimate secrets! Maybe it was because they knew that I was alone and a stranger, and that I would disappear somewhere together with their secrets. I heard Zosia's voice.

"Yes my husband lives in Lublin, but I won't get off there. I will hide and not disembark."

I could not understand it. "But you said that he wrote to you. Don't you love him? What happened?"

"He wrote. Yes, he wrote an eloquent letter—how he waits for me, how he remembers me. You know, I was beautiful," she said not without a trace of pride.

"You are beautiful," I told her sincerely.

"Have you seen my shoulder and my back?"

I then remembered seeing that her shoulder was bandaged. Oh yes—the boils that were the result of the malnutrition and other maladies common to so many people out here. They were hard to cure.

"Oh, that! They will heal."

"I've been trying to get them to heal for six months now. There are scars." She leaned over across the opening so that the moonlight shone on her. Slipping off the sleeve of her blouse and removing the bandage, I could see the red streaks even in the pale light.

"I'll show them to you in daylight. Then you will understand."

"But he loves you," I almost shouted. "What possible meaning could all of that—those scars on your back—have?"

"Shh, quiet!" she hushed me. Then she fell silent.

Again, we heard only the insane knocking and squeaking of the train. However, because of Zosia's words, the noise hardly penetrated my consciousness. I thought about love. I thought I knew all there was to know about both love and despair. Often I tried to imagine what it would be like to meet him once again, the man whom I would probably never see again. And even if by chance I did see him, surely he will have forgotten me. He was not my husband, not even my fiancé, just someone I loved and from whom I was forcibly separated. If I were to meet him again, I thought, would it possibly matter to me if he were disfigured?

Ah, but did I really know all there was to know about love? Were all those encounters, those conversations, those mutual infatuations, those meaningful silences, and even maybe those quarrels, were they only a romantic illusion? Was this—is this—all there is to love? How can it truly be love if it's not capable of withstanding a few years of separation and some scars on the body, or maybe even the soul?

"You are still quite young," Zosia said after a long silence. "Besides, everyone experiences love differently."

Zosia was quiet. I wanted to cheer her up somehow, but I also wanted to know more, I wanted to understand her. Moving closer to her, I said, "If he really loves you he won't discard you now, just when you've returned from exile."

"Oh yes…pity! Maybe out of pity he won't abandon me; he might even sympathize," she responded heatedly. "But I do not want pity. I don't want compassionate understanding. I love him, but I do not want pity binding him to me. Besides, he always treated me like a pretty plaything, an object whose beauty he enjoyed. You know, he was my professor. We all had crushes on him. He was so elegant and handsome and at the same time, older and unattainable. He had a reserved personality, a certain coolness and irony. So when he chose me I was happy—or maybe just proud —I'm not sure which. And even though we lived together, he was, in a way, always distant as if he were still my professor. He was proud of my looks, but he continued to live his own, somehow separate, life."

Zosia fell silent again. The steppe shimmered in the light of the setting moon. I was silent too, thinking about love. What was this thing called love? Maybe what I had experienced wasn't love at all—although how many years has it been now since that one man has filled my dreams? See how love is… it cannot stand pity. Actually, I wouldn't want him to love me only out of pity either….

Zosia went on, "I don't even know if, besides me, he didn't have another, more mature, more experienced woman. I was young and inexperienced. I didn't know much about husband and wife relationships. I wanted to destroy his impassivity, that perfection, that ironic sensibility. I wanted to replace all that with hot emotions. I wanted to force him to lose his composure but I never knew how to do that. So what can I possibly expect from him now, after seven years of separation and a scarred body?"

"Maybe you're wrong. Maybe he still loves you, maybe he can't wait to see you again, maybe he wants to be with you."

"No, no," Zosia answered quickly. "I can't take that chance. First, I have to recuperate somewhere and get my strength back. I want to appear before him healthy and whole, so he will not have to take pity on me. I'm older now; maybe I will know how to fight for his love, and not merely settle for his indulgence."

The steppe had darkened. It had gotten cold. We sat side by side in silence. Zosia gathered her blanket more closely around her, leaned against the doorway and I thought she was weeping.

Hers was not the only crying I heard in the boxcar. Someone else, off in a corner was sobbing too. Maybe someone was dreaming of an empty void with no one there to meet her. Or maybe it was someone who could not trust love and was afraid of meeting it?

On the brightening horizon, the sun rose to meet a new day, bringing us all closer to an encounter with the unknown.

Chapter 28:

In a Foreign City

I awoke. Out on the balcony doves were cooing. Beyond the open window, I could hear the sounds of a city that was waking up to a Sunday. Everything in the house was still. A clock's ticking deepened the silence. It was an unfamiliar silence. I was alone. I was in an unfamiliar house. Semi-awake, my thoughts came at me like dreams—or maybe I was still in a state of deep sleep. Doves cooed.

*   *   *   *

The winter morning is shrouded in twilight. I have to get up. My consciousness is still somewhere in its nighttime visions and reveries. Reluctantly, I relinquish the warm place in my bed; everything else is bitterly cold. The cat at my feet stirs irritably, stretches his paws, and rearranges himself into the warmed hollows of the blanket. I put on my sheepskin jacket and my valianky. My motions are only partly conscious.

I cross the semi-darkened tiny kitchen. The entryway is totally dark. During the night, snow has once more drifted halfway up against the door. Thin white streaks of snow, blown in through its cracks, appear on the entryway floor. I struggle with the door.

Outside, morning is breaking in the amber-colored light of the rising sun. A white cap of snow overhangs the eaves. I hesitate to disturb the fresh snow, as immaculate as the embodiment of beauty. Only wolf tracks, leading all the way up to the door, mar its perfect purity.

I step into the snow reluctantly and it shatters beneath my valianky. Its crystals shimmer. What a shame to ruin the gently sculpted figures on the protruding logs that I have to climb in order to reach the flat roof! Today even the chimney is wearing a snowy cap. It sits atop the straw pillow that I used to cover the smokestack last night to keep the stove-generated warmth from escaping.

For a minute, I stand motionless on the roof. This is my time of transition from a world of semi-consciousness to this next world of hard reality. I want to hold fast to this moment.

The village is silent; small gray puffs of smoke rise from white roofs. The sun, as if ensnared by the bitter cold, appears trapped within the intersecting rays of three small copies of itself. It's the intensely frigid and dense air at the horizon, acting like a mirror, which creates the three images of the sun. The sun itself is a crimson red, but it dyes the curls of smoke a vibrant pink and violet. Blushing in the cold, the horizon reddens.

Off in the distance, beyond these roofs I see the lone tree over the grave where my mother's body rests. There on the road far away, like miniature playthings, caravans of camels and ox-drawn wagons slowly start out across the steppe. I imagine that I hear (or maybe I really can hear them in this icy air) the squeaks of yokes and harnesses in the snow. The road disappears beyond the horizon. The steppe fades into a distant blue and endless space.

The frigid cold has penetrated my sheepskin jacket. I shiver and uncover the chimney.

With this action I have crossed the boundary from night into day. Now I must descend into the burdensome and harsh present with its people, its toil, its anxious uncertainties, its survival struggles—and its emptiness. So it will go until evening, when it ends here, in this same place, on this flat roof. Once more, the chimneys will spew their curls of smoke. The toy-like caravans will come back into the village. The sun will set, amidst biblical, gold-rimmed clouds, and with its crimson light, it will illuminate the lone tree in the cemetery where my mother rests.

But it may be that tomorrow, sometime during the day, out on the steppe the blizzard-demon will awaken. Unexpected, its first blows will come from the far beyond, from the distant hills. Soft snow-stars will turn into prickly pins. A shiver of horror will pass through the steppe in fear of the invading snowy horde. Low and treacherous at first, whistling softly, the blizzard will slide down from the hilltops into the village. Then its shrill blast will penetrate every crevice; it will shove, pierce and unsettle everything. Every human nerve will shrink in dread of all that is yet to come.

Its loud whistle will turn into a groan— and then into a wail. Ever louder, ever wilder, it will grow. It will flood the world, drown it out, confuse it, and lacerate each living nerve. It will seem to thrust its way into all recesses.

Then the snow-commandos, joining in its roar, will descend upon the earth. They will fly low at first; then gradually raising their heads higher and higher, they will sweep slowly, methodically, powerfully. They will impose layer upon layer of a thick impenetrable armor. They will force their way into entryways and past windows. They will destroy the soft forms of the previous night's snowfall and form their own densely packed, sharp, and layered strata. In some places, they will sweep the ground clean, down to its bare nakedness; elsewhere they will pile the snow up higher than a house—requiring entrance tunnels to be dug. Somewhere out in the steppe they may bury an entire caravan, or drive someone to distraction.

In the evening, I will go up on my roof by climbing atop the ice-covered log. Wrestling with the wind, I will cover the chimney. Nothing will be visible then, not the smoke from the neighboring houses, not the road with its caravans, not the tree in the cemetery where my mother sleeps. The snow-blizzard's cloud will cover everything.

I will not pause on the roof, as I do on peaceful evenings, to draw a quiet breath and mark the transition from one day to another; that will commence inside the house.

In our very own alternative world all these things—the thick walls of the unbaked- brick house with its low ceilings covered with rime, its central supporting pillar, its large baker's oven—become merely unreal apparitions.

Because then, at that moment, only that which is truly meaningful comes to life. See, here they are! Those that come to us from their graves and those that come from far away, those we left behind at home. They come to us as real living beings, intimately acquainted with everything we loved and knew and said and did and felt. They are here among us, more real and closer than the wind.

With them, our youth comes back to life; we seek each other's counsel, we weep, we love, we suffer together. We see our old home again with its daily bustle and its familiar smells, the trees in the yard, the clock on the wall, the furniture, the books….

There are two of us now and we summon back to life those who are closest to our hearts. We talk about them late into the night. The cat sits between us—wise like a sphinx, silent but comprehending everything.

This is where we truly live—until the next morning, which encroaches upon us with its daily struggles and desolation. This new present reality is just a bad dream; it's an illusion. That which we recollect is not merely a memory, it's a continuation, and it is hope.

*   *   *   *

All that was far away now. I woke up in a quiet house. The clock was ticking away. The doves were cooing. A dignified-sounding bell was tolling somewhere in the city.

This was not going to be a harsh day filled with struggles. This was the civilized soft reality of a city awakening to a new day. Still… there was emptiness. The city was pursuing its own life around me, past me. My soul was living amid memories, the tiniest traces of which I could not possibly find here. They had stopped being something closer than reality, they had become merely memories. And they stopped being hope.

I was in a foreign city and in an unfamiliar house. I felt emptiness.

Author's Note to the Third Edition

The idea of recording my experiences in Kazakhstan as a series of vignettes came to me in 1967 when I first came to the United States. V. Sofroniv-Levitsky, now living in Canada, was a well-known author, journalist, editor of the journal for which I worked in Ukraine just after I completed my studies, encouraged me to do so. My essays first appeared as a series of articles in the Canadian-Ukrainian newspaper, *Novyj Shliakh* (The New Way), of which he was the editor-in-chief.

Using Liubovych, my grandmother Hermina's maiden name (her married name was Shukhevych) as my *nom de plume*, the first edition of the collected essays appeared in 1969. That very year it won second prize in the Ivan Franko Literary Contest of Chicago. The book quickly sold out and I personally financed a second printing in 1972. The book was well-reviewed in Ukrainian diaspora press, but I was most gratified when a visiting writer from Ukraine told me that three copies of my book were circulating throughout Kharkiv in eastern Ukraine.

Especially meaningful to me were letters that I received from people whose knowledge of Kazakhstan was based on their own personal experience and who wrote that those who truly wanted to learn the truth about Kazakhstan should read my book.